FOR THE LOVE OF
CRYSTALS

Learn about the crystal's therapeutic properties and how you can use them to effect personal change.

This book is a wonderful resource for anyone, whether they are already well-versed in crystals or are just starting out on their crystal journey. Explore its contents to learn about the properties, uses, and energies that make each crystal special. The book also includes a supplementary chapter on building crystal grids, which can be used to channel the energy of crystals.

Just open to the appropriate chapter whenever uncertainty or curiosity strikes, and let the resonating energies serve your immediate needs. Keep this manual close, put your faith in itsadvice, and let its illuminating light lead the way. Go underneath the surface and discover your inner light.

Table Of
Contents

CHAPTER

1

INTRODUCTION TO

Healing with Crystals

1.1 THE SCIENCE AND SPIRITUALITY BEHIND CRYSTAL HEALING

If you look into crystal healing, you'll find a unique mix of science and spirituality, a dance of energy and purpose that works well together. At its core, crystal treatment is a form of medicine based on vibrations. It's the idea that everything, including you, moves at a certain frequency, from mountains to seas to you. These rhythms are the key to healing, balancing, and getting in tune with each other.

Imagine a world where gems and rocks aren't just pretty things to wear, but also useful tools. There are tools that have spiritual and healing properties that, when accessed and used, can lead to life-changing events. You don't need to wear a gemstone necklace or carry a crystal in your bag to feel its energy. When you put a crystal in a room, its healing energies spread through the room and affect the people in it.

Have you ever seen healers put stones on a person's body, lining them up along the spine or around the head? It's not just for looks; they are trying to keep the chakras and aura in order. Chakra might sound like a strange word, but it's just a Hindu word that means "spiritual energy." Ancient teachings say that our bodies have seven main energy areas or chakras and that each one has its own color.

It's interesting, right? How the levels of vibration in crystals and gemstones connect our spirit to the energy fields of the Earth. When you use a crystal, you want to boost or realign your mental or cosmic energy by letting its vibration guide it. Some doctors use crystals that match the color of each chakra to improve energy flow, while others prefer clear quartz because it can be used for so many things.

But, just like everything else, diamonds also need love. Think about how much weight the energy of the world would add to a rock. To keep it in its best shape, put it in salt water or cover it with table salt from time to time. Think of this as a spa day for your gem to clean it from "environmental imbalance." Just like you need time to relax and recharge after a long week, so do your crystals.

Crystals can do more than just balance energy; they can also pull out and get rid of broken energy from a person. By getting rid of the negative spiritual energy, they can ease both physical and mental pain. And crystal healers aren't the only ones who see this promise. Some nurses are using crystals as part of their overall care for patients. You can wear crystals, put them next to your bed, or even take a bath with crystals in it.

Crystals and people have been in love for a long time. We have been drawn to these shiny stones since the beginning of our species. We have used amulets, talismans, and gems for healing, protection, and spiritual direction. Crystal healers have been around for more than 10,000 years if you can believe it.

As we move further into a technological age, the desire for holistic treatment only gets stronger. More and more of us are becoming aware of other ways to be healthy, and diamonds are at the center of this movement.

As the world changes, keep in mind the power of crystals and how they bring order. No matter if you believe in crystal treatment or not, there's no denying that it's a fascinating blend of science and spirituality. If you jump in, you might find a whole new world of things you can do.

Since I can remember, I've always been drawn to the fascinating world of crystals. Their magic can't be put into words. Each part of their shimmer looks like it holds its own universe. I soon saw that I wasn't the only one who found this place magical.

After all, these sparkling gems are more than just fancy little things. They have a history and a charm that has been known and appreciated by many countries since the beginning of time.

Think about this: Our ancestors were just as amazed by these natural wonders thousands of years ago, before the digital age or even written records. They saw more than just stones. They saw tools, riches, and signs of mysticism.

Ancient Egyptians, for example, valued diamonds not just for how pretty they were, but also for what they thought were their spiritual and health benefits. Egyptian elites liked lapis lazuli because of its beautiful blue color, which was thought to keep away evil. People say that Cleopatra used powdered lapis lazuli as eyeshadow, not just for its beauty but also as a sign of power and respect for the energy of the rock.

In ancient China, jade was used in ceremonies to show purity and spiritual strength. It was also thought to attract love. The Mayans and Aztecs, on the other hand, respected gems like jade and turquoise and used them to make masks, statues, and burial objects.

In the Vedas, India's old holy books, there is a lot of information about how different crystals can be used for healing and spiritual growth. These early lessons are where the link between crystals and chakras can be found.

Who were the Greeks? The word "crystal" comes from the Greek word "krustallos," which means "ice." They thought that clear crystal was water that was always frozen. Many gems still have names and stories that reflect their language and beliefs.

Crystals have been appealing to people across countries and time periods, which shows how much people love these bright stones. They have been used to show power, help people get better, and even connect to the Holy. Throughout history, they have always been able to make people feel amazed.

Crystals are a reminder of how beautiful and mysterious the world is, whether it's because of their complicated shapes, bright colors, or the powers people think they hold. Everyone feels the same way I do about them because of their long and interesting history.

CRYSTALS IN OUR MODERN WORLD

The world moves so quickly these days that we often lose touch with nature's natural processes. The noise of modernity and social systems can make it hard to hear the quiet sounds of nature. As time has gone on, it's sad that we've often ignored nature's gifts.

The ruling patriarchal paradigms of the past didn't just shape political landscapes; they also stopped people from doing things that were seen as "feminine" or "earth-centered." Traditions based on natural healing or intuitive understanding were sometimes called "witchery" and pushed to the side. Crystal mending was one of the things that were pushed to the side.

But things are beginning to change. There is a strong desire to connect with our ancestors and find out what they kept hidden. Crystals, which have energies that don't change, are at the heart of this new movement. It's trip beyond nostalgia; it's a recognition that the past has tools for holistic well-being that modern people want.

The return of crystals can be seen everywhere, from yoga studios to psychiatrists' offices. They are reminders of both old knowledge and new needs.

On a personal level, crystals have changed my life for the better. In the chaos of life, they brought comfort and stability. Having them in my daily life was like seeing old friends again. They've become more than just friends; they keep me connected to the heartbeat of Earth and the vastness of the universe.

This comeback is not an isolated event. Crystals are said to have the power to change people all over the world. Whether or not there is scientific proof, the fact that crystals have been used for thousands of years and there are a lot of stories makes for an interesting story.

For me, getting into crystals was more than just going back to old ways. It was a conscious effort to reignite, resound, and harmonize. Crystals aren't just relics anymore; they're essential in a world where history and technology meet and where reason and faith coexist.

CHAPTER

2

GUIDING PRINCIPLES AND TECHNIQUES IN

Crystal Healing

2.1 CHOOSING THE RIGHT CRYSTALS: INTUITION AND KNOWLEDGE

It takes careful consideration to select the ideal crystal to meet your unique demands. It's a fine line to walk between using your own intuitive observations and basing your decisions on the fundamental understanding of each crystal's distinctive characteristics. This could appear difficult at first, but with a systematic approach, the process can be both illuminating and intensely personal.

Combining your innate, intuitive intuition with empirical knowledge is the essence of crystal choosing. This implies that while a part of you could be lured to the shimmer or feel of a crystal, a different part of you should be aware of its recognized qualities and previous applications. When these two selection criteria are combined, a decision is made that deeply reflects your conscious goals and inclinations.

DETERMINE YOUR INTENTION

Starting with a clear knowledge of your objective, choose a crystal. Consider your intended result or the energy you wish to welcome into your life before exploring the huge universe of crystals and their many properties. Are you looking for peace, or maybe courage, love, or clarity? By identifying your primary goal, you'll provide the groundwork for a more focused and potent crystal choice.

It's time to start doing some research after your purpose is clear as a bell (pun intended). Investigate the characteristics of numerous crystals, concentrating on those that are said to vibrate in accordance with your particular goal. For instance, if you seek inner peace and quiet, you'll naturally be drawn to crystals known for their relaxing properties. This phase is very important because it creates a synergy between your goal and the right crystal that might magnify the benefits you want to see.

The process is both reflective and educational. Your motivations and intents are personal, but you also follow the tried-and-true characteristics of each gemstone. This fusion of individual desire and ages-old wisdom creates the foundation for a potent and peaceful crystal experience.

CONNECT WITH THE CRYSTAL

When you're trying to find the right crystal, it's important to hold it in your hands or connect with it in your mind. You can start a silent chat between your energy and the energy of the crystal by holding it in the palm of your hand or even just imagining its weight and texture if you're looking at it online. This link, whether it's physical or mental, builds a bridge that lets the crystal's vibrations mix with your own.

Take a moment to settle yourself and say what you want to happen while you hold or think about the crystal. It's important to say what you want to happen in an upbeat and proactive way. Instead of thinking about what you want to avoid or get rid of, think about what you want to bring into your life. For instance, "I want inner peace" is a much more powerful statement than "I don't want to be anxious." This is because positive affirmations naturally line with the balancing vibrations of crystals. This makes it easier to channel and boost the energy you want.

TUNE INTO YOUR EMOTIONS AND BODY

It is important to get close not only to the crystal but also to your own physical and emotional reactions. Start by closing your eyes, turning off all outside noise, and being fully present in the moment. As you say what you want to happen, let the words echo inside you and pay close attention to how you feel. For people who are naturally in tune with their emotions, the crystal's vibration might feel like different things. You might feel incredibly light, or you might feel like your skin is buzzing. Some people say they feel elated, happy, or even get a sudden rush of energy. All of these are signs that the energy of the crystal is in tune with your purpose and vibration.

Muscle testing, on the other hand, can be very helpful if you are more aware of your physical self than your mental state. This method uses the body's natural responses to outside stimulation. To try this, stand with your feet about hip-width apart and hold the crystal or picture it in your mind if you're thinking of buying one online. Let your body move easily and watch to see if it naturally falls into a sway.

A crystal that leans forward usually means that its energy is in tune with yours, which could be a good sign. If, on the other hand, you find yourself leaning backward, this could mean that the stone isn't the best one for your wants right now. Muscle testing can be done in a number of different ways, and the sway method is just one of them.

The key to passing both emotional and physical tests is to keep an open mind and accept what your body and heart are telling you. These small signs will lead you to the best crystal alignment for your trip.

EMBRACE THE CRYSTAL'S INFLUENCE

Once you've found a crystal that feels right to you, you can consciously connect to its energy. When we interact with the outside world, we often try to keep outside factors from getting to us. This can sometimes lead to blocking out even good forces without meaning to. Stay aware and open to the energy of the crystal.

When you use both your intuition and your knowledge to choose crystals for healing, you get the most out of them and create a deeper, more harmonious relationship with these natural wonders.

Crystal grids are a beautiful mix of art, science, and faith. To just call them "arrangements" would not do them justice. In reality, these are cosmic plans that show the vibrational symphony of the universe through carefully chosen stones and a clear goal.

Each stone in a grid has a job that is like a note in a piece of music. A single crystal pulses at a certain frequency that can affect our physical and spiritual states. When it is in sync with other stones, the total power increases by a factor of ten. A group can move the whole universe, like a soloist in a band can move the heart. This idea is reflected in crystal grids, where the combined resonances of the crystals can cause big changes in health, manifestation, or spiritual growth.

But the power of a crystal grid doesn't just come from the crystals that are used. The foundational geometry, which is often based on sacred patterns like the Flower of Life or Metatron's Cube, works as a channel and amplifies the energy's path. Such patterns have been around for a long time and are respected across countries and time periods. By aligning crystals on these sacred geometries, we can tap into old knowledge, get in sync with cosmic rhythms, and use these powerful forces to reach our own goals.

Putting together a crystal grid is a complex dance of feeling and purpose. Stones are chosen not just for their own qualities, but also for how well they work with other stones. To do this, you have to be very sensitive to the quiet words of the stones. Once they are chosen, putting them on the grid becomes a sacred rite, a dance of fingertips and focused wishes that calls on, guides, and grounds cosmic energies.

In the end, a crystal grid is more than just a set of stones arranged in a certain way. It stands as a symbol of the beauty and interconnectedness of the world. A sign that the power of purpose, strengthened by Earth's treasures, can echo our deepest wishes across the universe. Using crystal grids can connect the real and the unreal, the personal and the cosmic, and offer changing experiences to both experienced practitioners and those who have never used them before.

If you want to go on this life-changing journey, the bonus chapter gives you a step-by-step guide that shows you how to make your own crystal grid, combining ancient knowledge with your own goals.

2.3 THE ENERGETIC INFLUENCE OF CRYSTAL JEWELRY

Crystal jewelry, whether in the form of necklaces, bracelets, earrings, or rings, has been cherished not just for its beauty but for its energetic properties. Across ancient cultures and even in today's modern world, these pieces have been believed to confer healing, protection, and various spiritual benefits to their wearers.

UNDERSTANDING THE ENERGETIC PROPERTIES

Each crystal has its own vibrational frequency, which is the same as that of the Earth it came from. This frequency works with the energy centers in the body, which are called chakras. It can help to align, clean, or even boost the chakras. Rose quartz, which is often called the "love stone" because it gives off vibrations of pure love, can be used to open and balance the heart chakra. Amethyst, on the other hand, has a calm energy that helps the third eye and crown chakras work better. This strengthens intuition and psychic connection.

WEARING CRYSTALS NEAR SPECIFIC CHAKRAS

Putting certain gems near the chakra they work with can make their effects stronger. When worn around the neck, a lapis lazuli pendant directly aligns with the throat chakra, which helps with speech and self-expression. In the same way, a citrine bracelet worn on the wrist can stimulate the solar plexus chakra, which can improve a person's sense of self-worth and personal power.

THE ROLE OF METALS IN CRYSTAL JEWELRY

Metals, while beautiful, can sometimes interfere with the vibrational frequency of certain crystals. This is especially pertinent when considering the energetic influence of crystal jewelry. Metals have their own unique energetic signatures, and when they come into contact with crystals, there can be either an amplification or disruption of energy.

For example, copper, known to enhance energy flow, can amplify the properties of crystals it's paired with. Silver, being a good conductor, can effectively channel the energy of crystals. However, metals like aluminum or even certain alloys may interfere with or diminish the energy of some crystals.

When choosing crystal jewelry, it's important to be mindful of the metal settings or clasps used. If possible, opt for pieces that use minimal metal or metals known to complement the crystal's energy, like copper or silver. Additionally, beaded crystal jewelry or pieces where the crystal remains largely in contact with the skin can also ensure the wearer receives its maximum benefit.

MAINTAINING YOUR CRYSTAL JEWELRY

Jewelry items require frequent cleansing just like loose crystals do to maintain their highest vibratory potential. They are exposed to a variety of energies throughout the day, which might cause them to develop negative energies or lose their energy. You can keep them powerful by performing regular moonlight cleansing rituals, burying them in salt, or utilizing smudging techniques. Use water sparingly, though, as some crystals can melt or degrade when exposed to moisture.

Jewelry made with crystals goes beyond simple fashion. It serves as a link between the underlying energies of Earth and our own energetic make-up. One can take advantage of the therapeutic, protecting, and transformative effects these lovely items have by picking the right pieces and caring for them properly. Personal intuition and attunement are essential in all spiritual and energy disciplines. When choosing and wearing crystal jewelry, use your intuition to make sure you're in tune with these priceless earthly gems.

3

CHAPTER

ESSENTIAL TIPS

3.1 PROPER STORAGE OF CRYSTALS

Storing your crystals properly is not only essential for preserving their physical integrity but also vital in maintaining their energetic vibrancy. Over time, crystals can accumulate energies from their surroundings or even from other crystals. Proper storage techniques can protect them from unwanted energies and potential damage.

HERE ARE SOME FUNDAMENTAL TIPS TO CONSIDER:

INDIVIDUAL POUCHES OR COMPARTMENTS
Avoid storing different types of crystals together. They can scratch or chip each other, especially if they have varying Mohs scale hardness levels. Utilize soft pouches or a segmented box to ensure they don't touch. This also prevents the mixing of their energetic frequencies.

NATURAL FABRICS
When choosing pouches, opt for natural fabrics like cotton, silk, or suede. These materials don't hold or transmit energies as much as synthetics do, ensuring your crystal's energy remains pure.

AWAY FROM DIRECT SUNLIGHT
Some crystals, like amethyst and rose quartz, can fade if left in direct sunlight for extended periods. Store them in a shaded place to maintain their color and energy.

STABLE TEMPERATURE AND HUMIDITY

Extreme temperatures and high humidity can be detrimental to some crystals. A cool, dry place, free from drastic temperature changes, is ideal. For instance, opals can lose their "fire" if they dry out, and selenite can degrade in high humidity.

SACRED SPACE

Create a dedicated space for your crystals, like a cabinet or shelf, that's cleansed regularly. This can serve as a sanctuary for your stones, keeping their energies clear and vibrant.

ENERGETIC CLEANSING

Even when stored, crystals can pick up ambient energies. Periodically cleanse them, using methods like smudging, moonlight baths, or sound therapy, to ensure they're energetically fresh and potent.

▪ LABELING

As your collection grows, it might become challenging to remember the specifics of each stone. Consider labeling them, especially if you have multiple varieties that look similar.

▪ GROUNDING STONES

To maintain balanced energy within your storage area, consider placing a grounding stone like black tourmaline, hematite, or shungite nearby. These stones help neutralize any unwanted or erratic energies, ensuring a stable environment for your crystals.

▪ USE TACT

Always handle your crystals with clean hands and a clear mind. Even when storing them, the energy you transmit can be absorbed. Ensuring you're calm and centered will prevent any negative energy transfer.

Your crystals will remain effective and durable if you store them properly. These are instruments for healing, change, and spiritual development, not just lovely stones. You can benefit from them for many years to come if you treat them with kindness and respect. Never underestimate the significance of the area and surroundings in which your crystals are placed, whether you are an experienced crystal healer or a novice.

3.2 CLEANSING TECHNIQUES FOR CRYSTALS

Crystals are more than just ornamental objects; they are powerful vibrational tools that interact and resonate with the energies around them. Over time, they can accumulate and store both positive and negative energies. Just as you would clean a physical tool after using it, it's crucial to energetically cleanse your crystals to ensure they function at their optimal vibrational frequencies.

Here are some popular and effective methods to cleanse and rejuvenate your crystals:

SMUDGING WITH SAGE OR PALO SANTO

How it works:
Smudging is a traditional Native American practice of burning sacred herbs to cleanse and purify a space or object.

Procedure:
Light the sage or Palo Santo stick until it smokes. Circle the crystal with the smoke, allowing it to envelop the stone completely. As you do this, hold the intention of clearing all negative energies.

MOONLIGHT BATH

How it works:

The light of the moon, especially during the full moon phase, is believed to have a purifying effect.

Procedure:

Place your crystals on a windowsill or directly outdoors under the moonlight overnight. The full moon's light will charge and cleanse the crystals, preparing them for further use.

SUNLIGHT

How it works:

Sunlight revitalizes and charges most crystals with radiant energy.

Procedure:

Place your crystals in direct sunlight for a few hours. However, be cautious, as certain stones like amethyst, rose quartz, and citrine can fade in prolonged sunlight.

EARTH BURIAL

How it works:

Burying a crystal taps into the grounding energy of Mother Earth, which purifies and recharges it.

Procedure:

Dig a small hole, place your crystal inside, and cover it with soil. Leave it for a day or longer, then retrieve and brush off the dirt.

RUNNING WATER

How it works:

Natural running water, like streams or rivers, can cleanse and recharge crystals.

Procedure:

Hold the crystal under running water for a few minutes while visualizing all negative energies being washed away. Note that some crystals, like selenite, shouldn't be submerged in water as they can dissolve.

SOUND HEALING

How it works:

Vibrations from sound can resonate with the crystal's structure, restoring its natural energetic frequency.

Procedure:

Using Tibetan singing bowls, tuning forks, or bells, produce a sound near your crystal. The vibrations will cleanse and re-tune the crystal's energy.

SALT WATER BATH

How it works:

Salt is a natural purifier, and its ions can pull away unwanted energies.

Procedure:

Mix sea salt into a bowl of water and place the crystal inside for a few hours. Ensure the crystal type can withstand salt and water exposure. Rinse with fresh water afterward.

REIKI OR INTENTION SETTING

How it works:

Reiki practitioners or those skilled in energy work can direct healing energy to cleanse a crystal.

Procedure:

By channeling energy through the hands and holding a clear intention, visualize the crystal being enveloped in a healing, white light.

USING OTHER CRYSTALS

How it works:

Some crystals, like selenite or clear quartz, can cleanse other stones.

Procedure:

Place the crystal needing cleansing on or near the cleansing crystal for several hours.

If you clean your crystals often, they will continue to help you on your spiritual and healing journeys. Just like you take care of your physical health, taking care of your crystals' spiritual health can make them work better and help you connect with them more deeply. As you try out these methods, keep in mind that the best one is often the one that speaks to you the most.

3.3 CHARGING YOUR CRYSTALS FOR MAXIMUM BENEFIT

After you've cleaned your crystals, the next step to making them more powerful is to charge them. Charging your crystals not only brings them back to life, but it also raises their vibrational frequencies and aligns them with your goals. This process makes sure that your crystal's energy is strong, alive, and in tune with your goals. Here are some useful ways to charge your crystals:

SUNLIGHT CHARGING

How it works:
The sun emits powerful energy that can invigorate and charge most crystals.

Procedure:
Lay your crystals out in direct sunlight for 2-4 hours. Note that some crystals, like amethyst, can fade in direct sunlight, so it's essential to research the particular requirements of each crystal.

MOONLIGHT CHARGING

How it works:
The phases of the moon, especially the full moon, emit a gentle, magnetic energy that can charge crystals.

Procedure:
Position your crystals under the moonlight, preferably during a full moon, and leave them overnight to absorb the lunar energy.

EARTH CHARGING

How it works:
The Earth's natural energy can ground and charge your crystals simultaneously.

Procedure:
Bury your crystals in the soil, as you would during cleansing. Leave them for 24 hours, allowing the Earth's magnetic field to charge them.

WATER CHARGING

■ **How it works:**
Natural bodies of water can harness both kinetic and magnetic energy to charge crystals.

■ **Procedure:**
If you're near a natural spring, river, or ocean, immerse your crystals for a few hours, letting the natural current envelop them. Remember, some stones, like selenite, are water-sensitive.

SOUND CHARGING

■ **How it works:**
Vibrational frequencies from sound can energize crystals.

■ **Procedure:**
Play tuning forks, singing bowls, or even certain frequency music (like 528 Hz) around your crystals. The resonating vibrations will charge them.

USING LARGER CRYSTALS OR CRYSTAL CLUSTERS

How it works:

Some crystals, such as clear quartz clusters or selenite slabs, can amplify the energy of other stones.

Procedure:

Place your smaller crystals on or beside the larger charging stone for 24 hours. The energy of the larger stone will transfer and amplify the smaller stone's vibration.

VISUALIZATION AND INTENTION SETTING

How it works:

Our minds are potent tools. By focusing our intent, we can channel and direct energy toward our crystals.

Procedure:

Hold your crystal in your hand or place it in front of you. Close your eyes and visualize a bright light enveloping the stone, charging it with vibrant energy. Speak or think about your intention for the crystal, cementing its purpose.

BREATH AND PRANA CHARGING

How it works:

The breath is a carrier of life force or prana. This energy can charge crystals.

Procedure:

Hold your crystal, take a deep breath, and as you exhale, direct your breath onto the crystal, visualizing your prana as a light or mist that envelops and charges the stone.

Utilizing your gems' full power requires regular charging. It equips them to work in accordance with your ambitions and goals. After use, charge them frequently to maintain the strength and efficiency of their vibrational frequency. You'll discover the techniques that work best for you and your crystals over time and with continuous practice, forging a link that only becomes stronger.

HOW TO USE COPPER TO ENHANCE CRYSTAL HEALING

Copper is a naturally found metal that is known for being a good conductor of both electricity and energy. Healers and shamans have known for hundreds of years that copper and crystals work well together in healing and energy work. This chapter goes into detail about how copper can be used to boost the power of crystals and how to make the most of this powerful combination.

WHY COPPER?

Copper's atomic structure makes it easier for energy to move through it. It works as a bridge or a way for spiritual energy to move back and forth between people, crystals, the environment, and the universe.

HIGH CONDUCTIVITY

In the realm of physics, copper is known for its electrical and thermal conductivity. Similarly, in metaphysical terms, copper is believed to amplify and transmit spiritual energy.

FREQUENCY ENHANCER

Copper can amplify the energy frequency of a crystal, making its effects more pronounced and easily felt.

BALANCING AGENT

Copper can balance the body's polarity or energetic alignment, helping to remove blockages and enhance overall well-being.

WAYS TO INCORPORATE COPPER IN CRYSTAL HEALING

COPPER WIRE WRAPPING

Wrapping crystals with copper wire not only secures them for jewelry but also amplifies their inherent energies. These wrapped pieces can be worn or placed in an environment to enhance the vibrational frequency of the space.

COPPER GRIDS

When laying out a crystal grid, consider using copper lines or shapes as pathways to connect the crystals. This fosters a strong, interconnected energy network that magnifies the grid's intentions.

COPPER PLATES

Resting your crystals on copper plates or slabs can keep them energetically charged. This method is particularly beneficial for those who regularly use crystals for healing or meditation.

COPPER AND ELIXIRS

Though copper metal should never be directly ingested, placing a crystal on a copper plate or surrounding it with copper while making a gem elixir can enhance the energy of the concoction.

COPPER MEDITATION RODS

Holding copper rods during meditation can help draw the energetic properties of any accompanying crystals deeper into your aura and chakras.

PRECAUTIONS WHEN USING COPPER

SKIN REACTIONS

Some people may experience a green discoloration on their skin when wearing copper. This is a natural reaction and not harmful, but if it causes discomfort, you might want to reduce direct contact.

NOT FOR INGESTION

Copper, especially in large amounts, can be toxic when ingested. Always ensure that copper does not come into direct contact with any elixirs or water meant for drinking.

CLEANING

Over time, copper can tarnish. Regularly clean your copper items to maintain their energy conductivity. Natural cleaning methods, such as using lemon or vinegar, can be effective.

Copper can be a powerful healing partner for crystals when it is used carefully and with respect. Its ability to enhance, transmit, and balance makes it a very useful tool for people who want to develop their energetic practices and make crystal healing work better. As with all metaphysical tools, you should trust your instincts and do study to find the best ways to use copper.

CHAPTER 4

DEEP DIVE INTO THE HEALING ASPECTS OF

Specific Crystals

AMETHYST

4.1 AMETHYST: THE STONE OF SPIRITUAL GROWTH

In the world of minerals, amethyst stands out as a beacon because of its intense purple color and the air of spirituality it gives off. Amethyst is a favorite among energy workers and spiritual seekers. It has historically been connected to the worlds of profound meditation and healing.

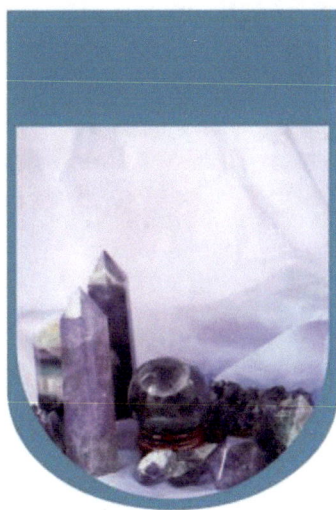

HEALING PROPERTIES AND USES

CENTERS ENERGY

Among its myriad attributes, amethyst's potency to center energy is especially revered. Many healers prefer to adorn themselves with amethyst jewelry, specifically necklaces set in silver, to harness its energy-balancing properties. When conducting healing sessions, it's not uncommon for the person receiving healing to clutch an amethyst stone, creating an energetic bridge between healer and receiver.

PHYSICAL HEALING

On a physical plane, amethyst is believed to offer therapeutic benefits, especially for conditions related to blood and respiratory systems. It's a common practice to place amethyst on affected areas, like the heart or lungs, aiming to channel its healing energy to these organs.

PURIFICATION AND PROTECTION

Amethyst clusters are a household favorite, serving as natural purifiers. By placing these clusters around your home, the ambient energy remains clean and positive, acting as a shield against negativity. In rooms where emotions may run high, strategically placing amethyst can instill an atmosphere of tranquility.

MEDITATIVE AID

The stone's calming influence makes it an exemplary companion during meditation. Holding amethyst can pave the way for intensified visualizations and a deeper connection to one's inner self. Its tranquil nature also aids in overcoming fears and managing cravings.

PSYCHIC ABILITIES

For those inclined towards psychic endeavors or possessing intuitive gifts, amethyst acts as a catalyst, augmenting psychic capabilities.

REMEDIES AND ELIXIRS

The amethyst's power isn't just limited to its physical form. By creating elixirs, one can harness its energies in liquid form. A popular remedy for migraines involves placing an amethyst on the forehead, allowing its cool, soothing vibrations to alleviate the pain. For respiratory challenges, positioning an amethyst over the chest can enhance breathing. Using the stone-infused water as an elixir can benefit skin health and boost circulation.

INSOMNIA AND DREAM WORK

Battling restless nights? Slipping an amethyst under your pillow might be the answer. Not only can it promote restful sleep, but it's also known to amplify dream frequency and clarity.

PROTECTION AGAINST THEFT

An age-old practice involves burying amethyst at entry points around the home, offering protection against potential intruders. This protective shield extends to keep malevolent energies at bay.

CONNECTING WITH THE DIVINE

Amethyst can serve as a bridge to higher realms. Holding the stone during spiritual sessions can facilitate a deeper communion with one's Spirit Guide or Higher Self, fostering a sense of unity with the universe.

STRESS RELIEF

In an ever-accelerating world, stress has become an unwelcome constant. Just a few moments with amethyst can offer a respite, rejuvenating the nervous system and ushering in peace.

Amethyst is an essential stone in the spiritual community because of its lengthy history and variety of applications. Amethyst promises to be a dependable ally, illuminating the road to spiritual advancement whether you're a healer, a fan of meditation, or someone seeking calm and protection.

APATITE

4.2 APATITE: ENHANCING ONE'S INSIGHT AND CLARITY

With its diverse properties, apatite has long been acknowledged as a stone that encourages acceptance and transformation. It stands out among gemstones as a sign of equilibrium, communication, and inner and outer harmony.

CHAKRA BALANCING

Regardless of which chakra is in question, apatite showcases its versatility. Whether it's reinvigorating a dormant chakra or pacifying an overstimulated one, apatite ensures a harmonious flow of energy.

UNLOCKING PSYCHIC ABILITIES

For those on a spiritual quest, apatite acts as a catalyst, unlocking dormant psychic abilities. It harmonizes the mind, heart, and soul with the ethereal vibrations permeating the cosmos. To enhance foresight and envision future occurrences, placing an apatite – preferably of blue or purple hue – against the third eye chakra can be immensely beneficial.

PHYSICAL HEALING

On a physical plane, apatite proves to be a boon, particularly for bone health. By aiding calcium absorption from consumed food, it ensures the robustness of bones and teeth. For those battling arthritis, securing an apatite stone against the affected joint can potentially expedite the healing process and alleviate pain.

ELIXIRS AND REMEDIES:

Crafting an elixir with apatite is simple. Place the stone in water and let it imbibe lunar energies overnight, ideally during a full moon. Consuming this elixir can fortify bones and mitigate joint discomfort.

HYPERTENSION MANAGEMENT:

To regulate high blood pressure, positioning an apatite stone near the heart is recommended. An apt method would be to wear it as a pendant. However, if that's not feasible, discreetly attaching it inside one's attire can work just as well.

EMOTIONAL AND LOGICAL BALANCE

In high-pressure situations, emotions can often eclipse logic. With apatite as an ally, one can maintain a serene demeanor, allowing rationality to guide the way.

FOSTERING CREATIVITY

Apatite can be an artist's best friend. Donning this gemstone can kindle the creative spark, leading to the creation of masterpieces.

OVERCOMING SOCIAL HURDLES

Feelings of shyness or apprehension in social scenarios can be disheartening. Apatite promises to infuse the wearer with confidence, ensuring they radiate their authentic self in social gatherings.

BOOSTING MOTIVATION

Sometimes, all one needs is a nudge to see tasks to completion. Meditating with a gold or red apatite can instill focus and drive, ensuring the task at hand gets the attention it deserves.

Apatite offers remedies for problems in the physical, emotional, and spiritual spheres in all of its varied hues and forms. This stone is ready to help, pointing people in the direction of a balanced and meaningful existence, whether they are looking for inner peace, physical healing, or a stronger connection to the universe.

GREEN SERPENTINE

4.3 GREEN SERPENTINE:
AWAKENING KUNDALINI ENERGIES

A stone with strong earthly vibrations, green serpentine encourages meditation and raises consciousness. It is a lighthouse for individuals exploring the spiritual world.

SPIRITUAL ELEVATION

A quintessential tool for spiritual ascent, serpentine activates the crown chakra, bolstering psychic abilities. Its vibrational energies ensure that individuals remain grounded while they explore the ethereal dimensions, fostering a deeper understanding of life's spiritual essence.

KUNDALINI AWAKENING

Serpentine not only reveals new paths for the ascension of the Kundalini energy but also ensures its harmonious movement. This stone, embedded with ancient wisdom, can also help access memories from past incarnations, ensuring a profound connection with one's soul lineage.

EMOTIONAL AND MENTAL STABILIZER

Serpentine is akin to an anchor in tumultuous waters. It rectifies emotional and mental imbalances, guiding the healing energies precisely where they're required. With the serpentine's guidance, one can harness the innate power to lead a life with renewed purpose and direction.

PHYSICAL DETOXIFICATION

A powerful detoxifier, serpentine's influence extends to the physical body, purifying the bloodstream and ensuring vitality. Its properties combat parasites, optimize calcium and magnesium absorption, and offer therapeutic benefits for conditions like hypoglycemia and diabetes.

ANGELIC CONNECTIONS WITH LIGHT-GREEN SERPENTINE

The gentle hue of light-green serpentine is a gateway to the angelic realms. For those seeking divine guidance, this variant of serpentine proves to be invaluable. It seamlessly knits the tapestry of past, present, and future, making it an ideal companion for past-life regression.

HEALING EMOTIONAL TRAUMAS

Beyond its striking appearance, the light-green serpentine is a balm for the wounded soul. It propagates self-compassion, urging individuals to embrace and heal the scars from past traumas. It's particularly potent in addressing unresolved issues, ensuring emotional baggage from bygone relationships is addressed.

EXPRESSION AND RESOLUTION

When placed on the throat chakra, light-green serpentine aids in vocalizing repressed emotions and memories. Its presence ensures any confrontations with figures from the past occur with grace, facilitating understanding and resolution.

PHYSICAL ALLEVIATION

The curative properties of light-green serpentine are unparalleled, particularly when it comes to alleviating pain. Whether it's menstrual discomfort or muscular tension, this stone offers relief, restoring harmony to the body.

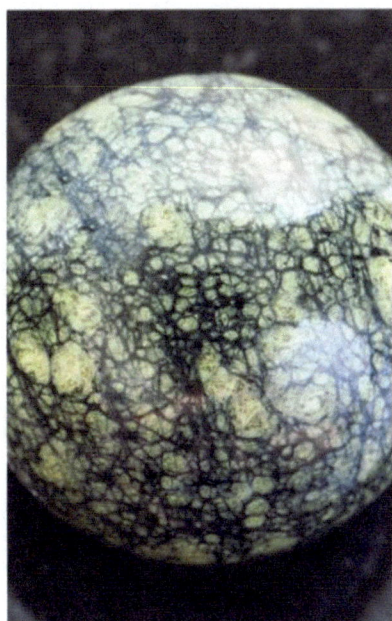

In all of its shades, green serpentine is more than just a piece of rock. It treats the spiritual, emotional, and physical aspects of existence holistically. Whether one is pursuing spiritual progress, bodily healing, or emotional equilibrium, green serpentine is a dependable ally, promoting health and spiritual development.

TURQUOISE

4.3 TURQUOISE: SKY STONE AND SPIRITUAL GROUNDING

Turquoise, sometimes known as the "sky stone," is a symbol of the long-standing bond between people and the vastness of the cosmos. This diamond is revered not only for its physical beauty but also because it serves as a spiritual link between our life on earth and the higher planes of consciousness.

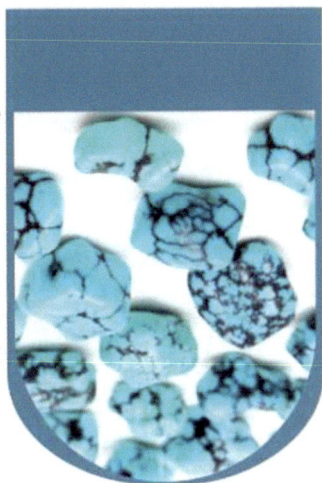

UNDERSTANDING SELF

Turquoise illuminates the path to self-awareness. It nudges us to introspect, to find tranquility in silence, and encourages us to embrace our true essence. Its energies guide us in understanding our thoughts and emotions, thus paving the way to personal power and growth.

SACRED PROTECTOR

For cultures like the Native Americans, turquoise wasn't just a gemstone—it was an embodiment of divine energy. Its innate properties absorb negative energies, transforming them into positivity and clarity. It's as if the gem is inviting its possessor to tune in to the universe's vastness, to resonate with its harmonies.

DIVERSE HEALING ATTRIBUTES

Turquoise's multifaceted healing prowess caters to the individual needs of its users. Whether you wear it close to your skin or meditate with it, the gem stands as a sentinel, guarding and rejuvenating the spirit.

ALIGNING THE ENERGY CENTERS

To achieve balance and harmonize one's energy systems, turquoise can be used to align the chakras. By placing a turquoise stone on each chakra, one allows the gem's energies to recalibrate the body's energy centers, ensuring a free flow of vitality and wellness.

PHYSICAL DETOXIFICATION

Beyond its spiritual qualities, turquoise serves as a protector of our physical being. Wearing a loop of turquoise beads is believed to act as a purifier, detoxifying the body from pollutants, toxins, and negative influences, be it from alcohol, the environment, or even radiation.

RESPIRATORY RELIEF

Those plagued with respiratory ailments, or conditions like asthma, can benefit from turquoise's healing properties. Wearing the stone close to the affected area ensures its potent energies address the root of the issue, fostering healing and relief.

EMOTIONAL BALANCER

Depression, often a culmination of negative energies and suppressed emotions, can be alleviated with the consistent influence of turquoise. It serves as a beacon of hope, dispelling the shadows of despair and inviting light into the soul.

TURQUOISE ELIXIR

DepThis powerful elixir, formed by immersing turquoise in water bathed under the sun and moon, is a panacea for a myriad of ailments. From soothing headaches to healing injuries, strengthening immunity to mending tissues, the elixir captures the gem's essence, offering its curative benefits in a tangible form.

The ethereal blue-green color of turquoise serves as a symbol of the awe of nature and serves to remind us of our sacred relationship to the cosmos. It functions as a healer, a guardian, and a compass. We discover comfort, clarity, and a call to go farther in our spiritual ascent in its embrace. Whether you're looking for mental clarity, emotional stability, or spiritual development, turquoise, in all its celestial splendor, is ready to be your companion.

THE QUARTZ SPECTRUM

4.4 THE QUARTZ SPECTRUM

The venerable crystal quartz is frequently referred to as the "Master Healer." The adaptability and prowess of quartz have remained unmatched, from the ethereal worlds of legendary ancient civilizations like Atlantis to the precise instruments in contemporary modern equipment. Its pervasiveness in both the spiritual and scientific spheres attests to its profound qualities.

THE SCIENCE BEHIND QUARTZ

At the very foundation of this crystal lies its unique crystalline structure that can transmit electricity and radio frequencies. This property explains its ubiquity in our electronic devices, from radios to watches. Modern science is continuously exploring the depths of quartz's potential, speculating it could be the key to revolutionary alternative energy sources.

QUARTZ DIVERSITY

Amongst the quartz family, each variant is unique, each resonating with specific healing vibrations that influence different parts of the human system. While all types of quartz realign the body's vibrations and restore balance, rose quartz and clear quartz are particularly prominent in the spectrum.

ROSE QUARTZ

Often termed the 'Stone of Unconditional Love,' rose quartz exudes an aura of compassion, love, and tranquility. It's the go-to stone for emotional healing, fostering self-love, and forging deeper relationships.

■ HEALING PROPERTIES

Crystal healers swear by rose quartz for alleviating headaches, fortifying the heart, and enhancing kidney function. Emotionally, it aids in healing the scars of the past, promotes forgiveness, and ushers in self-acceptance.

■ ENERGETIC RESONANCE

Its gentle pink essence vibrates at a frequency that aligns with the heart chakra, making it an indispensable tool in heart-centered meditation and healing rituals.

CLEAR QUARTZ

As the name suggests, this stone is all about clarity. It's a potent amplifier, known for its ability to boost the energy of other stones and intentions.

■ HEALING PROPERTIES

Clear quartz is a multi-dimensional healer. From drawing out pain and cleansing the aura to amplifying curative energies, its spectrum of abilities is vast. It serves as an anchor, grounding wandering energies and clarifying consciousness.

ENERGETIC RESONANCE

Connecting with the crown chakra, clear quartz facilitates a stronger link between the physical dimension and the higher realms of consciousness. Its lucidity mirrors its purpose—to grant clarity to thoughts, intentions, and visions.

THE SILICA CONNECTION

Rose quartz and clear quartz are both good for healing because they are made of silica. The energy frequency of these crystals is amplified when silica is combined with silicon, which is known for its electromagnetic properties. Silica is found in almost every healing gem, which shows how important it is in the world of crystal healing.

As we look at the different kinds of quartz, it becomes clear that these crystals are more than just rocks. They are energy beings that connect the earth to the universe. Rose quartz, with its heart-centered energies, and clear quartz, with its luminous brightness, are proof that nature has the power to heal, harmonize, and raise the human experience. Embracing these timeless gems is like tuning into the love and clarity of the universe's music.

CITRINE

4.5 CITRINE: THE MERCHANT'S STONE AND PERSONAL WILL

Glistening with the golden hues of a sunlit morning, citrine is the epitome of brightness and positivity. Dubbed the "Merchant's Stone", it's not only an attractor of wealth and prosperity but also a beacon of inner strength and self-confidence. Just as the sun chases away shadows, citrine dissipates negativity and gloom, making way for hope, joy, and abundance.

ECONOMIC AND SPIRITUAL PROSPERITY

The moniker "Merchant's Stone" was not bestowed upon citrine lightly. Throughout history, merchants have kept this stone in their cash registers, believing in its ability to draw wealth and success. But beyond its economic significance, citrine's true wealth lies in its spiritual richness. It's a gem that fortifies one's personal will, propelling individuals to manifest their dreams and transform them into reality.

MENTAL CLARITY AND CREATIVITY

Citrine is like a burst of sunshine for the mind. It enhances concentration and revitalizes the mind, making it excellent for overcoming depression, fears, and phobias. Creatives hail citrine as a muse, for it awakens the imagination and propels one into uncharted territories of creativity.

PERSONAL WILL AND CONFIDENCE

Linked with the third chakra, the solar plexus, citrine boosts self-confidence and initiative. It's a gem of manifestation, empowering you to overcome obstacles, make decisive choices, and take assertive action on your dreams.

DETOXIFYING AND REVITALIZING

Physically, citrine is a powerhouse. It's known to regenerate the body, aid in digestion, and cleanse the spleen and organs of elimination. Its detoxifying properties also extend to the emotional and mental realms, assisting in releasing pent-up emotions and thought patterns that no longer serve.

PROTECTIVE AURA

Citrine's radiant energy does not just attract positivity; it also repels negative energies and guards against negativity of all kinds. Wearers often find that they are better shielded from external negative influences, making citrine an excellent stone for sensitive individuals.

Using citrine in everyday life can change things for the better. Citrine is a powerful stone that can be used in many ways. You can put it on your desk to attract professional success, wear it close to your skin to use its protective aura, or meditate with it to gain awareness and personal power.

Citrine stands out as a bright thread that tells stories of wealth, personal strength, and happiness. It's not just a stone; it's a sign of the rich opportunities we all have inside us. By using the energy of citrine, we not only attract wealth from the outside, but we also enrich our inner world. This strengthens our personal will and shows us the way to our greatest potential. Accept citrine and let the sun in you shine brightly.

AMETRINE

4.6 AMETRINE: BALANCING THE MIND AND SPIRIT

Imagine the warmth of the sun meeting the gentle caress of twilight; that's ametrine for you. A stunning blend of amethyst's serenity and citrine's vibrant energy, ametrine is nature's testament to the beauty of duality and harmony. It's a dance of fire and water, capturing the imagination of both seasoned gem aficionados and spiritual seekers. Ametrine offers a balanced path between the mind's logic and the spirit's intuition, making it an unparalleled guide for life's journey.

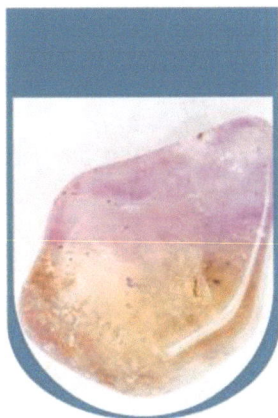

DUAL ENERGETIC PROPERTIES

Born from the heart of Mother Earth, ametrine is a unique gemstone that naturally combines two distinct energies. The golden warmth of citrine promotes personal power and invigorates the body, while the calming lilac shades of amethyst instill peace and enhance spiritual awareness.

MENTAL AND SPIRITUAL HARMONY

Ametrine is particularly beneficial for those seeking to bridge their analytical side with their intuitive senses. It encourages clarity of thought while also boosting psychic and spiritual insights. This makes decision-making a more holistic process, considering both logical assessment and intuitive guidance.

CREATIVITY AND TRANSFORMATION

Melding the energies of both its parent stones, ametrine stimulates creativity and supports transformational shifts in one's life. Whether you're an artist searching for inspiration or someone looking for the courage to embark on a new life path, ametrine is a steadfast ally.

EMOTIONAL BALANCE

By integrating the mind and spirit, ametrine also fosters emotional equilibrium. It dispels negativity, reduces stress, and helps one overcome anxieties by maintaining a balanced perspective.

ENERGIZING AND CALMING

Reflecting its dual nature, ametrine has the unique ability to invigorate the spirit while also grounding and calming the mind. This means you can harness its energy during meditation for both focus and expanded consciousness.

To use all of ametrine's energies, you can meditate with the stone to improve your mental visions while staying grounded in the present. Wearing ametrine jewelry keeps its balancing energies close by, so you can get a steady flow of its power all day long.

Ametrine is a rock that shows the way to balance in the world of gems. It reminds us that two things can live together in harmony, and that embracing both our intellectual and spiritual sides gives us a lot of power. As we move through the rough waters of life, ametrine acts as a compass, guiding us toward balanced decisions, mental resilience, and a deep, integrated understanding of who we really are. When we embrace ametrine, we open ourselves to a symphony of forces that work together to improve both our earthly and spiritual lives.

BLOODSTONE

4.7 BLOODSTONE: THE STONE OF COURAGE AND HEALING

Bloodstone is like the life force that flows through our blood. It has a unique deep green color with bright red spots. In the past, it was called heliotrope, and its history is as deep and mysterious as its looks.

HISTORICAL SIGNIFICANCE
Rooted in ancient lore, the bloodstone was said to control the forces of nature. Tradition held that when submerged in water under the sun's rays, it possessed the formidable power to summon storms.

GATEWAY TO CREATIVITY AND EXPRESSION
Bloodstone has been linked with unlocking latent creativity and nurturing individual expression. Its energizing properties inspire innovative thinking, breathing life into art and other creative ventures.

A MEDICINAL MARVEL
The Middle Ages witnessed the bloodstone's esteemed medicinal applications. Ground into powders or transformed into pastes, these preparations were believed to treat a plethora of ailments, from tumors to bleeding wounds.

CIRCULATORY HARMONY

The stone's name alone hints at its profound connection to blood. Healers have often turned to bloodstone for treating blood disorders, emphasizing its capacity to address issues like anemia, circulation challenges, and even complex conditions like Lupus.

A GUARDIAN OF IMMUNITY

Not only does the bloodstone act as a fortifying agent for the circulatory system, but it also bolsters the immune system, detoxifies vital organs, and ensures the purity of the body's core components. This makes it particularly beneficial for women, offering relief during menstruation and menopause.

ANCIENT DIVINATORY PRACTICES

Bloodstone, with its distinct red specks, became a conduit for psychic visions for ancient Babylonians. The stone's unique patterns would be interpreted to gain insights into the future or understand mysterious occurrences.

MOONLIT REJUVENATION

Harnessing the full moon's power, a ritual with the bloodstone could purify the individual. This nocturnal meditation, with the stone placed on the forehead, would draw lunar energies, dispelling negativity and ailments.

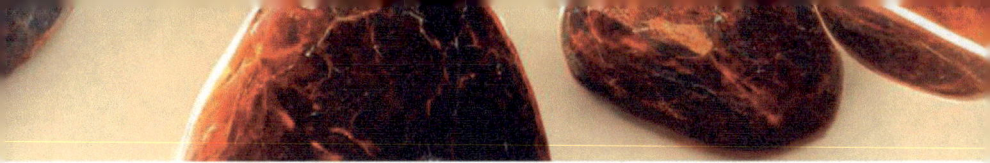

BOLSTERING BRAVERY AND ATHLETIC PROWESS

The Egyptian warriors of yore wore bloodstone amulets to enhance their strength during battles. Today, athletes and anyone in need of a confidence boost can turn to the bloodstone's invigorating energies.

ENHANCED PERCEPTION AND GENEROSITY

A bloodstone's grounding energy can help shift perspectives from self-centered views to a more holistic understanding, fostering empathy and compassion.

JOURNEY TO PAST LIVES

This stone, during meditative states, acts as a gateway to previous lifetimes, aiding one in accessing memories and experiences from past lives.

PROSPERITY'S MAGNET

Stationing a bloodstone at workspaces or areas of financial transactions can attract wealth and growth, amplifying opportunities for prosperity.

Bloodstone is a great example of how much the Earth can heal, strengthen, and inspire. Bloodstone is still a highly valued spiritual and metaphysical tool, whether it's used to increase physical energy, clear the mind, or pave the way to spiritual awakening.

SHUNGITE

4.8 SHUNGITE: THE MIRACLE STONE OF HEALING

Shungite, with its deep, lustrous black appearance, is more than just a stone; it's a millennia-old guardian of health. Hailing from the Karelian region of Russia, this enigmatic mineral has woven its way through legends, often revered for its profound healing attributes.

ANCIENT ORIGINS

Shungite is believed to be over two billion years old, making it one of the most ancient minerals on Earth. Its existence predates organic life, bearing witness to the very birth of biological evolution.

FULLERENES – NATURE'S MARVEL

Shungite's notoriety in the healing community is largely due to its unique molecular structure. It's one of the very few natural sources of fullerenes – a rare, hollow carbon molecule. These fullerenes are known for their ability to neutralize free radicals, thus making shungite a sought-after mineral for promoting health and combating environmental toxins

A SHIELD AGAINST ELECTROMAGNETIC FREQUENCIES (EMFS)

In our tech-dominant world, we're constantly exposed to electromagnetic frequencies from our devices. Shungite acts as a protective barrier against these EMFs, safeguarding our well-being and enhancing mental clarity.

PURIFICATION ELIXIR

Ancient civilizations and modern communities alike recognize shungite's water purification capabilities. By simply placing this stone in water, harmful bacteria and contaminants are believed to be neutralized, rendering the water cleaner and more invigorating.

ENERGETIC BALANCER

Rooted in its deep black color, shungite is associated with the base or root chakra. It aids in grounding energies, stabilizing emotions, and fostering a connection to the Earth.

A BALM FOR THE BODY

Traditionally, shungite has been used to alleviate a myriad of physical ailments. From easing joint pains and skin conditions to revitalizing the body's energy flow, its therapeutic benefits seem boundless.

GUARDIAN OF THE PSYCHE

Shungite isn't just a physical healer. It's also believed to protect against negative energies or psychic attacks, paving the way for emotional balance and spiritual growth.

RESTORATIVE SLEEP AND DREAMS

Placing shungite near the bed or under the pillow can induce a peaceful sleep. It's calming energies can deter nightmares and potentially promote lucid dreaming.

RECHARGING AND CLEANSING

Like other stones, shungite absorbs negative energies. It's advisable to regularly cleanse and recharge this mineral, ensuring its optimal healing capabilities. Basking it under moonlight or sunlight or placing it on a bed of salt can rejuvenate its powers.

Shungite, often dubbed the "Miracle Stone," is indeed a marvel of nature. Its multifaceted healing properties, both tangible and esoteric, make it an indispensable asset in holistic healing practices. Whether it's safeguarding our health, promoting emotional equilibrium, or acting as a spiritual beacon, shungite remains a testament to Earth's benevolent gifts to humanity.

PYRITE

4.9 PYRITE: THE STONE OF ABUNDANCE AND PROTECTION

Often mistaken for gold due to its metallic luster and golden hue, pyrite, also known as "Fool's Gold," is more than just a mineral. It's a beacon of prosperity, protection, and personal power.

HISTORY AND ORIGINS

Named from the Greek word "pyr" meaning "fire," pyrite can create sparks when struck against metal or stone. This fiery nature has made it an emblem of ignited passion, determination, and creativity throughout history.

VIBRATIONS OF WEALTH AND ABUNDANCE

Pyrite's golden gleam is symbolic of its energies. It's renowned for attracting abundance, wealth, and prosperity. By channeling the assertive energies of the Earth and Sun, pyrite bolsters one's willpower and drive, pushing one towards success and fulfillment.

PROTECTIVE SHIELD

This mineral isn't just about wealth in the materialistic sense. Pyrite also serves as a shield, deflecting negative energies, environmental pollutants, and physical danger. It's a guardian stone, watching over those who harness its power.

ENHANCING MENTAL PROWESS

Pyrite stimulates intellectual capabilities, enhancing memory, and promoting quick thinking. It's the ideal stone for students, researchers, and those in mentally-demanding professions, bolstering clarity and focus.

HARMONIZING THE ENERGIES

At its core, pyrite is a harmonizer. It aligns the energies of the body, fostering emotional well-being, and balance. It helps dispel feelings of inadequacy, instilling confidence and a can-do attitude.

PHYSICAL HEALING ATTRIBUTES

Traditionally, pyrite has been associated with healing properties beneficial for the respiratory and circulatory systems. It's believed to purify the body, encourage better oxygen supply, and boost overall vitality.

SOLAR PLEXUS CHAKRA RESONANCE

Connected to the Solar Plexus chakra, pyrite enhances one's personal power and inner strength. It helps in overcoming inferiority complexes and boosts self-worth.

GROUNDING AND EARTH CONNECTION

Its deep connection to Earth makes pyrite a grounding stone. It anchors the user, ensuring stability and a connection to the planet's nurturing energies.

ENERGIZING SPACES

Placing pyrite in a workspace or home attracts positive energy. It not only stimulates the flow of wealth but also infuses the environment with its vibrant, uplifting energies.

CARING FOR PYRITE

Pyrite, being metallic, can tarnish over time. Keep it away from moisture and store it in a dry place. Occasionally cleansing it under moonlight or smudging with sage can help maintain its radiant energy.

Pyrite, with its golden allure, is a reminder that treasures aren't just material but also spiritual. It champions ambition, protects against harm, and fosters a spirit of abundance in all aspects of life. A stone of many facets, pyrite truly shines in its role as a guardian and harbinger of prosperity.

FLUORITE

4.10 FLUORITE: SPIRITUAL WHOLENESS AND UNITY

Known for its breathtaking range of colors, fluorite is often referred to as the "Gemstone of Discernment.
Its varied palette, from purples and greens to blues and clear, mirrors its ability to inspire clarity, unity, and elevated thought.

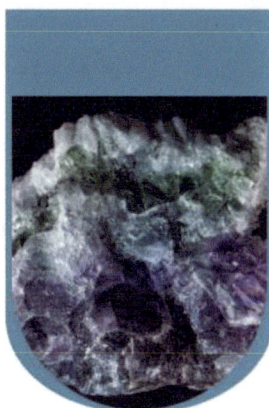

HISTORY AND ORIGINS

Fluorite, derived from the Latin word "fluere," meaning "to flow," has been cherished for centuries for its stunning beauty and luminosity. Ancient Egyptians and Chinese incorporated fluorite into statues and amulets, valuing both its aesthetics and its perceived spiritual attributes.

A SPECTRUM OF SPIRITUAL GROWTH

Each color of fluorite offers unique energies. While purple fluorite increases spiritual balance and intuition, green fluorite heals heart chakra, aids access to intuition, and clears negative energy from any environment. Blue fluorite calms the mind and fosters orderly thoughts, and clear fluorite acts as a clarifier and cleanser of energy.

GUIDING MENTAL ENHANCEMENT

Fluorite is particularly known for its resonance with the mind. It sharpens focus, balances the cerebral hemispheres, and augments one's ability to integrate and process information. For students or professionals, it's a boon for concentration and clarity.

HEALER OF THE HEART AND AURA

Fluorite, especially in its green shades, connects deeply with the heart chakra, encouraging harmony and the beneficial flow of heart-centered emotions. Furthermore, it cleanses and stabilizes the aura, repelling negativity and stress.

PROMOTING UNITY AND RELATIONSHIP HARMONY

In relationships, fluorite fosters understanding and connection by aligning the energies of everyone involved. It bridges the gap between head and heart, ensuring decisions are made with a balance of intellect and emotion.

PHYSICAL HEALING POTENTIAL

Historically, fluorite has been believed to act as a powerful healer, particularly in areas related to bone health, arthritis, and pain relief. Its calming energies can also help alleviate stress-related disorders.

THIRD EYE AND CROWN CHAKRA CONNECTION

Fluorite stimulates the Third Eye, heightening psychic intuition, and establishing strong links to spiritual realities. When connected to the Crown Chakra, it fosters a sense of divine connection and unity with the universe.

PROTECTION AGAINST ELECTROMAGNETIC FOG

In our digital age, fluorite stands as a protective barrier against electromagnetic smog, making it an excellent stone to keep near electronic devices.

BALANCING POLARITIES

In its essence, fluorite balances - whether it's harmonizing two differing viewpoints, aligning the spiritual and physical, or bringing equilibrium to chaotic energies.

CARING FOR FLUORITE

Being a softer gemstone, fluorite needs gentle care. Protect it from scratches and avoid exposing it to rapid temperature changes. Clean it with mild soap and water, and recharge its energy under moonlight.

Fluorite serves as a beacon of higher consciousness and spiritual completeness because of its fascinating colors. For individuals seeking oneness, clarity, and spiritual development, it is a stone that cannot be without due to its profound ties to the mind and spirit. Fluorite is a guide and a protector, whether you're looking for harmony in your relationships, need mental clarity, or are on a spiritual search.

OBSIDIAN

4.11 OBSIDIAN: THE STONE OF TRUTH AND PROTECTION

Obsidian is a glassy, dark stone that emerges from the extreme heat of volcanic eruptions. It is created when lava cools quickly. Its dark, reflecting surface acts as a potent mirror, ability to inspire clarity, unity, and elevated thought.

ANCIENT ROOTS AND SIGNIFICANCE

The name obsidian traces back to Obsius, an ancient Roman who allegedly discovered it in Ethiopia. Throughout history, from Mayans to Native Americans, obsidian has been crafted into sharp tools, ceremonial blades, and talismans of protection.

PEELING AWAY ILLUSION

Regarded as the "Stone of Truth", obsidian brings clarity by revealing shadows, fears, and hidden emotions. It urges one to face these hidden aspects, facilitating deep self-reflection and growth.

THE PROTECTIVE WARRIOR

Resonating with protective energy, obsidian acts as a spiritual guard, deflecting negativity and shielding its bearer from psychic attacks. Its grounding nature helps to anchor erratic energies, making it a vital tool for spiritual cleansing.

EMOTIONAL AND MENTAL HEALER

Obsidian aids in identifying patterns that need transformation. By bringing these to light, it fosters emotional healing, helping release pent-up feelings and trauma that have been held back, facilitating clarity and inner peace.

ROOTED IN THE EARTH

Obsidian, with its grounding properties, connects one to the Earth's energies, fostering balance and stabilizing one's foundation.

PHYSICAL PROTECTOR

Beyond its spiritual and emotional benefits, obsidian is believed to aid digestion and detoxification. It is said to reduce arthritis pain, joint problems, and cramps.

SHARPER THAN THE SHARPEST BLADE

In ancient times, obsidian was chiseled into blades sharper than steel. This sharpness is not only physical but metaphysical. As a stone, it slices through illusions, revealing one's deepest truths and vulnerabilities.

PURIFICATION RITUALS
Used in shamanic ceremonies, obsidian can cleanse auras and rid the environment of spiritual pollutants.

A COMPANION DURING TIMES OF CHANGE
Obsidian's transformative nature makes it a trusted ally during transitions, ensuring that change is for the best.

CARING FOR OBSIDIAN
While obsidian is relatively hard, it can get scratched. Cleanse it with warm water and mild soap, and energize it under the moonlight or through smudging.

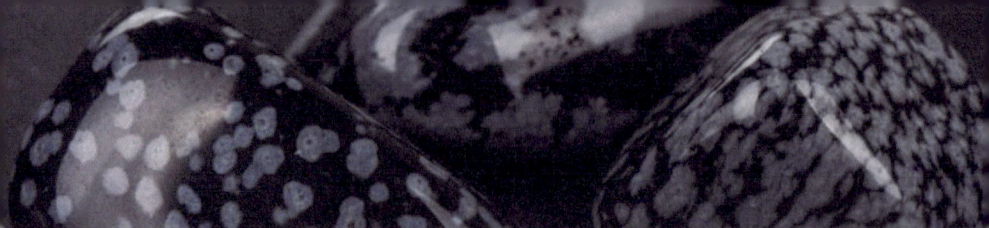

VARIOUS FORMS AND THEIR UNIQUE POWERS

SNOWFLAKE OBSIDIAN
Speckled with white patches, this form brings balance to mind, body, and spirit, resembling the serene snowfall on a dark night.

RAINBOW OBSIDIAN
When polished, this variant displays beautiful iridescent layers. It is believed to heal the heart and offer hope through its colors.

MAHOGANY OBSIDIAN
This reddish-brown obsidian enhances strength, offering protection during challenging times.

As a protector and a leader, obsidian is present. Obsidian offers unmatched security and profound wisdom for individuals prepared to confront their inner realities and embrace change, despite the fact that its dark, reflecting surface may be intimidating to some. It is essential for those looking for the truth and pursuing personal development since it acts as a mirror to the soul and a defense against difficulties.

BLACK TOURMALINE

4.12 BLACK TOURMALINE: THE ULTIMATE PROTECTION STONE

Black Tourmaline, often regarded as the sentinel of the crystal world, has long been venerated for its its unparalleled ability to ward off negative energies. This stone, with its enigmatic dark hue, encapsulates protective qualities that are unrivaled, making it indispensable for both spiritual and physical well-being.

HISTORICAL BACKGROUND

Its name is derived from the Sinhalese term "turmali," which was a term used for various gemstones found in Sri Lanka. For centuries, black tourmaline has been a talisman of protection against curses, threats, and negative intentions.

REPELLING THE UNWANTED

As one of the most potent protectors, Black Tourmaline safeguards its wearer or environment from harmful electromagnetic frequencies, psychic attacks, and all forms of negativity, transforming them into positive and harmonious energies.

GROUNDING PROPERTIES

Intrinsically tied to the Earth's energies, black tourmaline offers grounding properties that stabilize and fortify one's emotional and physical state. It forms a bond between the Earth and the human spirit, ensuring a balanced aura.

SPIRITUAL HEALING

For those embarking on spiritual journeys, black tourmaline acts as a compass, guiding its user and providing a barrier against lower energies and destructive forces. It is also instrumental in promoting the transformation of dense energy into a lighter vibration, aiding spiritual growth.

CLEANSING AND PURIFICATION

Black tourmaline has the remarkable ability to transmute negative energies, purifying one's surroundings. Its cleansing properties are not just spiritual; it also aids in detoxifying the body and balancing the chakras.

ENHANCING PHYSICAL WELL-BEING

Reputed to boost immunity and provide protection against environmental pollutants, it's a beacon for those seeking holistic wellness. Black tourmaline has also been associated with improving circulation, supporting liver function, and ensuring the health of the immune system.

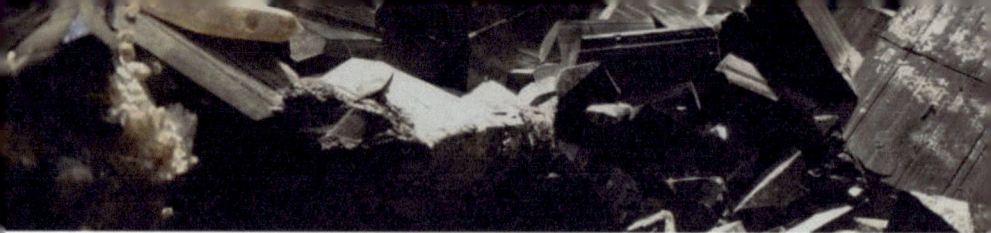

DEFLECTING ELECTROMAGNETIC FREQUENCIES (EMF)

In our digital age, Black Tourmaline stands as a protective barrier against the harmful effects of EMF. Keeping this stone near electronic devices ensures that their radiation is neutralized.

EMPOWERMENT AND CONFIDENCE

Beyond protection, Black Tourmaline is known for bolstering self-confidence, diminishing fears, and promoting an objective view of situations, fostering a positive attitude even in challenging times.

HARMONIZING ENERGIES

Working harmoniously with other crystals, it amplifies their positive energies while providing an envelope of protection. Many spiritual practitioners combine Black Tourmaline with stones like Selenite to augment its protective capabilities.

CARING FOR BLACK TOURMALINE

It is essential to cleanse this stone regularly, considering its capacity to absorb negativity. Smudging or placing it on a selenite slab can effectively cleanse it. While it's robust, it's best to keep it away from harsh chemicals and prolonged exposure to sunlight.

Black tourmaline isn't just a stone; it's also a watchful guardian who keeps an eye out for the person who owns it. With Black Tourmaline by your side, you'll always be protected, rooted, and shielded from negativity, whether you're venturing into spiritual worlds or just getting through your day-to-day life.

5

THE COSMIC CONNECTION: ELEMENTS, PLANETS, AND CRYSTALS

A delicate ballet of energies is taking place in the vastness of the cosmos. Inherent to our spiritual constitution are the stars, planets, and elemental forces; they are not only far-off things. Crystals act as conduits in this cosmic ballet, connecting us to these innate forces and enabling us to tap into their energies

EARTH

Earth is the place where all life starts and gets its purpose. This basic force, which is the same as the calm and steady color green, represents life in its most natural state. Deep in the center of this elemental resonance, we find crystals, which are nature's jewels and are made of the spirit and vibrational essence of the Earth.

EARTH

Out of all these crystalline wonders, Jasper stands out as a symbol of security. It looks like the solid rock that our world is built on. It makes you feel like you're strongly rooted, like an old tree whose roots go deep into the Earth's crust. In the same way, Green Aventurine, which sparkles with hope, brings about growth and wealth. It tells us to plant the seeds of our goals and care for them with patience and care, knowing that they will grow into fruit in their own time.

With its intricate designs that look like lush forests, Moss Agate acts as a link between the heart and the gifts of nature. It gives people a safe place to go, a way to return to Mother Earth's arms and feel better. In its embrace, we are told that life is cyclical, that the seasons change and that people die and are born again. This gem, along with its elemental brothers and sisters, becomes a sign of peace and stability in a world where time is always changing.

As we go through the many things life has to offer, the Earth element and the crystals that protect it serve as our guide. They tell us where we came from, give us a sense of security when things are uncertain, and push us to live in harmony with the natural world. In their quiet, long-lasting presence, we find a place to hold on to our hopes and dreams and a constant reflection of the beauty and strength of our world.

AIR

As our sensations rise from the solidity of the Earth, they reach the ethereal warmth of the Air element. Air, which has a bright yellow glow, stands for the vastness of the mind and the constant flow of thoughts that go through it. It is where ideas come from, where imagination takes flight, and where the mind can dance freely. Here, in this world of endless clouds and passing breezes, we are asked to think, dream, and look for answers that go beyond the physical.

AIR

The crystals that echo the energy of the sky are at the center of this elemental fabric. Citrine, with its yellow shine, acts as a catalyst to wake up the mind and make things clearer. It tells us to let go of self-doubt and open ourselves up to the light of information and self-awareness. Yellow Calcite, a stone known for its soft sound, is traveling with Citrine. It helps sort out complicated feelings and helps us say what we're feeling in a clear and graceful way, like a poet weaving words into poems.

With its many levels, Tiger's Eye gives the Air's ethereal essence a sense of stability. It makes us smarter by improving our intuition and showing us the way to understanding. Just as the wind can carry seeds to new places where they can grow, these air-aligned diamonds help us see things from a different point of view. They teach us how to listen, not just to the people and things around us but also to our own thoughts.

When we connect with the Air element, we are told to go beyond our limits. With the help of its guardian crystals, we learn to navigate the realms of logic and emotion, to interact in an honest way, and to appreciate the vast landscapes of our minds. It's a warning that our thoughts and ideas, like the wind, have the power to change the world, lift us up, and give us hope.

FIRE

As we come out of the whispering winds of the Air element, we are then wrapped in the fiery hug of the Fire element. This strong force, which shines with a bright ruby red light, is a sign of the wild spirit of passion, drive, and raw energy. The essence of fire, which reminds us of old campfires and molten lava, is a strong way to channel physical strength, spark our deepest desires, and lead us on our way with the certainty of a blazing trail. It's not just the warmth that keeps us safe from the biting cold, but also the spark of life that gives us strength to do everything we do.

FIRE

Garnet is one of the most important rocks that remind us of this power of nature. Its deep color, which reminds us of the heart of an ember, rekindles our spirits and emotions. It's not just a stone; it's a call to action that tells us to face problems with the same passion and determination as a fighter going into battle. Next comes the earthy presence of Red Jasper, a gem that, even though it is linked with the fire's strength, acts as a stabilizing force. It's a warning that even in the middle of a raging fire, there is a stable center, a grounding force that makes sure our flames stay steady and don't go out or flare up out of control.

Then there's Fire Agate, which has a mesmerizing dance of bright patterns that look like they've captured the very soul of a flame. With its swaying warmth, this stone gives us energy and makes us more determined. It tells us stories about old fire gods and urges us to use our natural abilities and shape our futures with a strong will.

The Fire element shows us how important it is to be persistent and how desire has the power to change things. With the help of its guardian rocks, we can learn how to use our energy in a positive way, work hard to reach our goals, and embrace the warmth and strength that are already inside of us.

WATER

When we leave the fiery intensity of the Fire realm, we find ourselves in the soft embrace of the Water world. This domain, which is painted with the deepest blues of the ocean and the calm colors of peaceful lagoons, shows how our feelings are always changing, just like the tides that come and go on our planet's shores. With its gentle persistence, water can shape and mold the Earth, and our feelings can do the same to us, pushing us to think, change, and grow. In this watery world, aquamarine jumps out as a bright gem. Its clear blue depths remind us of the calming vastness of open water and help us get clear and think about ourselves.

WATER

When we hold an aquamarine, we're not just holding a stone; we're also holding a promise of peace and understanding that goes back hundreds of years. It seems like the seas, with their many secrets, are whispering stories of bravery, strength, and inner peace. Lapis Lazuli, a gem with the depth and wonder of the night sky, is another peaceful light in this vast body of water. Rich and luxurious, it tells us of how complicated our emotional world is and how many things we can do when we accept ourselves.

Then there is Blue Calcite, a stone that looks like the soft moving of kelp forests in the ocean or the gentle caress of a river. Blue Calcite can help heal mental wounds and give you the strength to go through tough currents because of its nurturing energies. Its presence whispers a theme of balance, telling us to find balance in our feelings and be grateful for both the highs and lows.

The fluid ease and deep depth of the Water element remind us of how beautiful and important our emotional journey is. It shows how important it is to understand, accept, and handle our feelings with care and bravery. With the help of the crystals' guiding lights, we are given the tools to dive deep into our emotional waters and find knowledge, love, and self-awareness.

THE PLANETS

As we look up from the earth to the stars, Mars, with its fiery red color, jumps out as a symbol of bravery and strength. Crystals like Red Coral and Bloodstone reflect this strong energy and give us the strength to face obstacles head-on. With its bright yellow glow, the Sun gives us energy and strength. Crystals like Sunstone, Amber, and Gold Calcite shine strongly, like the sun in the morning. They can help us heal and be successful.

THE PLANETS

Jupiter is the spiritual giant of our solar system. It is covered in deep purple colors. It tells you how to meditate and become psychically aware. Gems like Amethyst, Charoite, and Sugilite help us tap into this expansive energy and expand our mental horizons. Mercury, who wears yellow and moves quickly, is in charge of communication and knowledge. Mercury makes us smarter and better at communicating through rocks like Agate, Amazonite, and Sodalite.

But this isn't the end of the cosmic link. Venus, which has shades of pink and green, is in charge of love and peace. Rose Quartz, Emerald, and Rhodonite all reflect the magnetic pull of this world, making it easier for people to connect deeply and understand each other. Saturn's stern energy, which is shown by dark blue or black colors, is a sign of discipline and duty. Obsidian, Black Tourmaline, and Lapis Lazuli help us remember what we've learned in life and how important it is to do our duties.

To know about the world is to know about yourself. Our soul moves in the same way as the elements, planets, and crystals. As we align ourselves with these forces, we find that every cosmic turn brings us growth, healing, and change. Accept this trip and let the world show you the way.

CHAPTER

6

THE POWER WITHIN: USING CRYSTALS FOR

Inner Strength

6.1 HARNESSING THE ENERGY OF FIRE TO COMBAT FATIGUE

Fire, with its fiery shades of bright red, is not only a sign of warmth and light, but also of an endless flow of energy. This element, at its core, fights against the chains of tiredness and provides a safe place for people who want to rekindle their inner spark. Crystals, which are thought to have special powers in many cultures, have a lot in common with this fiery element. Most importantly, crystals that pulse with hot energy often have ties to the Sun or the planet Mars. These crystals are easy to spot because they tend to be red.

When we talk about Mars, it has a powerful, determined energy that has earned it the respected name "Planet of Warriors." It is a symbol of this warrior spirit and a call to all people who feel worn down by life's many obstacles. For one must call on and use their inner warrior's strength and fortitude to fight off fatigue.

The Ruby is one of these gems that has this fierce force in its very core. Its deep, crimson color is just as captivating as the Fire and Mars powers that are thought to be in it. Ruby is a strong stimulant, so it doesn't just sit there and look pretty; it does something. By improving blood flow and increasing stamina, it works as a source of new, re-energized energy. It is said to heal when put on the sacral or root chakra, especially when it is in its raw form. To keep it healthy, you must take care of it by gently cleaning it and letting it bask under a starry sky.

Still, Mars has more to give than just Ruby. Garnet is another gem that shows the fiery desire of the planet. It shines a deep burgundy-red color, connecting it to both the Fire element and the planet Mars. When this stone touches the root chakra, magic happens: the slow circulation is sped up, and a dying desire for life is rekindled. Garnet is a simple stone that can be worn as jewelry or kept close in a bag. Even on cloudy nights, its energy doesn't go away. It's always ready to recharge and start over.

But while Mars is the fighting planet, the Sun is the source of all energy that makes life possible. Amber is another rock that has this same life force. Amber is a fascinating stone because it is made from the fossilized remains of old tree resin. Its golden-orange beauty not only draws the eye, but also goes well with the fire element and the brightness of the sun. Its real power, though, is in how it can refresh and lift you up. Amber gets her energy back up by encouraging a cheerful attitude. When feelings threaten to get too much, a smart placement on the solar plexus or sacral chakra can help a lot. Like any valuable gem, amber does best when it is taken care of. Putting it on a sunny shelf will keep it charged and ready to give its user warmth and energy.

6.2 ALLEVIATING EMOTIONAL FATIGUE

Emotional tiredness is common, but we often don't pay enough attention to it. Many people think that tiredness only means being physically tired, but being emotionally tired can be just as draining. Emotional overload is as real as any physical illness. It can show up as sleeplessness, deep sadness, or even depression. And just like we look for cures for physical problems, certain crystals stand out as signs of hope in the midst of this mental chaos.

Amethyst, with its calm purple color, is more than just a pretty stone. It is also a healing gem. This crystal has been used for healing for a long time because it is in tune with the ethereal element of air and the vast energy of Jupiter. People who are emotionally worn out often find comfort in the calming hug of the amethyst. Not only does it soothe the soul by getting rid of sleepiness and headaches, but it also helps keep things in balance, especially with blood sugar levels. It's interesting that its healing powers don't just work on itself; they also work on other stones nearby.

You don't have to do a lot of complicated practices to tap into its powerful energies. Just putting something on the brow chakra can make a big difference. Putting it under your pillow can help you get a good night's sleep if you're looking for comfort. But like all beautiful and powerful things, it needs to be taken care of. The amethyst grows best in the soft light of the moon, where it can recover. But you should be careful about putting it in full sunlight, as that could weaken its powerful effects.

Aventurine, on the other hand, has a soft green color that brings out the energy of the Earth. Its effect, which is also changed by Mercury, is a unique mix of steadiness and communication. Aventurine is a beautiful stone, but it also protects against bad things. In its presence, negative thoughts are replaced by a growing sense of hope. Its gentle, energizing nature can give people a new spark for life, especially if they have been feeling down because of mental fatigue.

Aventurine is easy to use, and its impacts are also very strong. When put on the heart chakra, it works like a shield, keeping away anxiety and the feeling that emotional stress is too heavy to handle. For its powers to stay strong, it needs to be refreshed every so often. An easy way to do this is to hide it in the leaves of a plant during the day. This link with nature not only gives the aventurine energy, but it also makes it feel more connected to the earth.

6.3 FIGHTING AFTERNOON LULLS

The afternoon break is something that many people go through. As the day goes on after lunch, we often feel tired and need a boost to get through the rest of the day. Many people's first response might be to reach for a cup of coffee or a sugary snack, but there is another, more holistic way to deal with stress if you look deeper.

Ruby, with its fiery red color, is the very definition of rebirth. It is a rock that is very close to the element of fire. It stores energy that is ready to be used. When you start to feel tired in the afternoon, this powerful stone acts as a lighthouse, waking you up and energizing your spirit. Its lively energy not only wakes up the body but also sharpens the mind, making sure that work done after lunch is done with the same enthusiasm as work done in the morning.

Along with Ruby, Amber is a sign of how powerful the old world was. This golden-orange gem, which is mostly preserved tree resin, channels the ancient energy of the Sun. When the weight of the afternoon starts to drag someone down, Amber lifts them up and gives them back their lost energy. In addition to giving you more energy, it also resets your mental compass, making you more optimistic and positive, even when you have a lot to do.

Jasper is a calming force, even though it is not as fiery as Ruby or as bright as Amber. It adds to the energy-giving effects of the other two by stabilizing the person and making sure that the new energy doesn't fade away quickly. This balance is important, especially during the workday, so that people can be productive without getting burned out.

Last but not least, Aventurine needs to be mentioned. It's not a powerhouse of energy, but it's a big part of how you feel after lunch. Its soft, green glow makes us feel good, so that as our energy is restored, our attitude stays hopeful and bright. After all, during a busy day, it's not enough to just fight fatigue; we also need to keep our spirits up, so we can face problems not only with energy but also with a smile.

6.4 PROMOTING RESTFUL SLEEP

As we try to relax in our beds at the end of the day, exhaustion can sometimes play a cruel trick, leaving our bodies tired but our thoughts constantly busy. It's strange that the very tiredness we want to get away from keeps us from getting a good night's sleep. When this happens, the world offers whole-person solutions that have been around for a long time.

Rose Quartz and Amethyst are two gems that are known to help people sleep. Their peaceful energies fit perfectly with the soft feelings we feel when we're dreaming. Rose quartz is often called the "stone of universal love" because it makes people feel peaceful and helps heal the heart from the stress of daily life. Amethyst, on the other hand, with its soothing purple color, is a calmer stone that gets rid of restlessness and makes it easier to relax. Those who have trouble sleeping may find that putting one of these gems under their pillow helps them fall asleep and stay asleep.

Rose Quartz and Amethyst are both good for helping you sleep, but Blue Lace Agate adds a little something extra. With its intricate designs and soft blue tones, this stone makes you feel calm. It does more than just help people fall asleep; it also helps the body reach a deep state of rest. When you're feeling tense, just holding this gem can be like taking a deep, quiet breath, resetting your body's rhythms.

Then there's Iolite, which is great for the modern mind, which often has too much knowledge. Besides looking beautiful, this gem helps calm minds that are stressed out. It can help with a wide range of problems, from sleeplessness and eyestrain to headaches that won't go away. Iolite is especially useful because it can ease mental stress and calm frayed nerves. It's a haven for the senses in a world where things are always happening.

In the end, managing the complex dance of life, whether it's the highs of adrenaline-filled activities or the lows of boring routines, requires tools that help keep you in balance. Whether you're a competitive athlete or just trying to deal with the stresses of everyday life, there's a crystal waiting in the wings to help you get back on track. Here's to embracing these treasures from the past and moving into a world of renewed energy and peace that can't be found anywhere else.

CHAPTER

7

INTEGRATING CRYSTALS INTO

Healing Sessions

7.1 SETTING INTENTIONS AND PREPARING THE SPACE

When it comes to healing sessions, using crystals can significantly enhance the results and experiences for both the healer and the recipient. Their organic vibrations, hues, and energies blend together beautifully with different healing treatments. However, utilizing these jewels calls for planning, preparation, and comprehension.

Setting clear intentions is essential before starting a therapeutic process. Intentions serve as a compass for the session's energies, ensuring that they are directed toward the desired result. When it comes to crystals, a healer's intention can guide and refine their intrinsic energies. For instance, selecting a crystal with heart-centered energy, like Rose Quartz, and programming it with the aim of emotional release would be ideal if the session's objective is to promote emotional healing.

Equally important is the space's preparation. A calm and orderly setting not only allows for the free flow of energy but also guarantees that the recipient is at ease and receptive to the experience. Clean up the area first. Smudging with sage or utilizing musical instruments like singing bowls or tuning forks are examples of traditional techniques. The objective is to remove any leftover negative energies from the area.

Place the selected crystals in the area after that. Consider laying up a crystal grid on the ground or all the way around the healing table, which can serve as an energy matrix and direct the vibrations of the crystals in a particular pattern. Depending on the treatment modality and your desired outcome, this grid can be as simple or complex as you like.

Make sure the room's components are in balance. A potted plant or other earthy element might help to ground the area. While a basin of water might signify fluidity and emotions, a flickering candle can conjure the fire element, which stands for transformation. Last but not least, fresh air— possibly through an open window—can keep the energies revitalized and moving.

The healer must also take time to center themself. The healer's energy can be brought into alignment with the intention set for the session by a brief grounding exercise, meditation, or even a few deep breaths. By taking this step, the healer can channel the healing energy without any personal obstacles getting in the way. Recall that these stones are our traveling companions as we learn more about the integration of gemstones into therapeutic sessions. They freely provide their vibrations, and when they are handled with respect and compassion, their potential for healing is absolutely limitless.

7.2 COMBINING CRYSTAL HEALING WITH OTHER MODALITIES

With its long history and built-in energy manipulation powers, crystal healing is not the only holistic therapy out there. The power of both can be enormously increased when used in conjunction with other healing techniques, providing a multifaceted approach to wellbeing.

REIKI AND CRYSTALS

Reiki is an old way that comes from Japan that uses the universal life force energy to heal. A Reiki practitioner transfers this energy into the body, mind, and spirit by putting their hands in certain places. Reiki is an all-around way to get healthy because it focuses on balancing the chakras, which are the energy areas in our bodies. But when mixed with the power of crystals, Reiki becomes much more powerful and can bring about a deep change.

Crystals are gifts from the Earth, and people have respected them for hundreds of years for their unique vibrational patterns and healing powers. Each type of crystal has its own benefits because it resonates with a different frequency that can heal, clean, or energize. When these natural vibrational levels meet the energy that is being channeled during a Reiki session, the healing experience is made stronger. They boost and direct the Reiki energy, making it easier for it to move through the chakras.

Consider the deep purple amethyst, which is known for its calming effects and link to the third-eye chakra, the place where intuition and foresight come from. When this crystal is put in a certain way on the third-eye chakra during a Reiki session, it not only boosts the Reiki energy but also opens up the chakra. What happened? Clearer thinking, deeper thoughts, and a stronger sense of intuition.

The Amethyst isn't the only rock that works well with Reiki. There are a lot of different crystals, and each one has its own special qualities that can be matched to different chakras or healing needs. For example, a Rose Quartz can be used to open the heart chakra, which can help with love and mental healing. For the root chakra, you could use a grounding stone like Black Tourmaline to help you feel more stable and connected to the Earth.

Both Reiki and crystals have a lot of power on their own, but when they work together, they make a powerful healing method. By knowing how each crystal is different and how it interacts with Reiki energy, practitioners can offer a more complete, deep, and personalized healing experience.

ACUPUNCTURE AND CRYSTALS

Acupuncture is an old Chinese medical technique that has been used for thousands of years to fix problems with the flow of energy in the body. Acupuncture is based on the idea of Qi (pronounced "chi"), or life force. To stimulate, redirect, or balance this vital energy, thin needles are inserted at specific meridian spots. Each of these places is a gateway that affects different organs, feelings, or body functions.

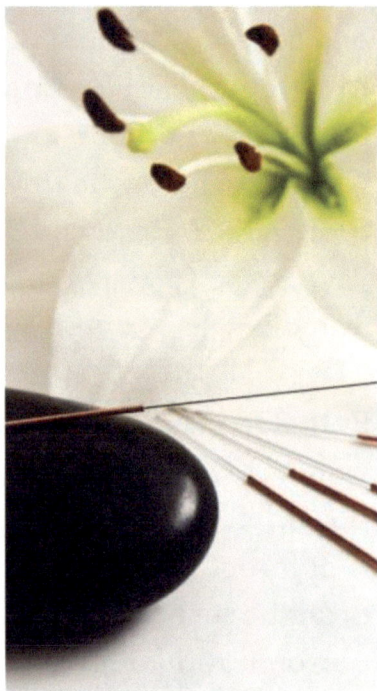

Now think about combining this old method with the powerful vibrational energy of crystals. Because each crystal has its own frequency and healing qualities, it can be used to boost the effects of acupuncture. When carefully put along the meridian lines or near the acupuncture points, these stones can speed up the flow of Qi and boost the healing effects.

Think about Clear Quartz, which is often called the "master healer" of crystals. It can receive, store, and release energy because of its clear, prismatic shape. When used with acupuncture, it can make the treatment work better by making the flow of Qi through the meridian spots stronger. This improvement not only speeds up the repair process but also makes it better at what it does.

Selenite is another powerful rock that is known for its ability to clean and charge. By putting Selenite along the meridian lines, it can be used as a purifier to get rid of blocks and make sure energy flows more smoothly and without interruptions. This makes sure that each acupuncture point gets a clean, strong dose of Qi, which makes the treatment work better.

In essence, when acupuncture and crystals are used together, they offer a complete way to heal. Acupuncture focuses on the body's internal processes and how energy moves through them. Crystals, on the other hand, add an outside force that helps this process. This collaboration, which is based on old healing methods, has the ability to help people heal faster and more deeply.

MASSAGE THERAPY AND CRYSTALS

With its long past, massage therapy has always been a beacon for people who want to get rid of aches, pains, and tension in their bodies. Massage therapists use their skills to move the soft parts of the body in ways that help people relax, get more blood flowing, and feel better overall. But what if this practice, which is already helpful, could be made even better? Walk into the world of crystals.

The natural vibrational frequencies of crystals give them a wide range of healing qualities. When used with massage, they increase the benefits of the session, working not only on the physical level but also on the mental and energetic levels. This integrated method takes advantage of the fact that the body works as a whole, making sure that the healing is complete.

Warm stones, in particular, have been a popular massage tool for a long time. For example, Basalt is a rock. The iron in these volcanic stones makes them very good at keeping heat. When heated and put in the right places on the body or used as an extension of the therapist's hands, they reach deep into the muscles. Together, the warmth and the energy of the stone work to loosen muscle knots and clear energy paths that have become blocked.

Himalayan salt stones are another popular choice, and they bring more to a massage than just heat. When heated, these pink stones release negative ions that help balance the body's electric field. They are known for their ability to clean the body. When the therapist moves these stones over the skin, they not only relax sore muscles but also help clean and balance the body's energy, which makes the person feel clear-headed and calm.

The combination of massage treatment and crystals shows how effective it can be to use both traditional methods of physical healing and energetic healing methods together. This link between touch and energy works well together to create a deep, multidimensional healing experience that affects all parts of a person's health.

SOUND HEALING AND CRYSTALS

Sound healing is an old technique that has always been interesting to people who are interested in the healing power of vibrational frequencies. Practitioners use tools like sound bowls, tuning forks, and gongs to make waves of sound that match the body's natural frequencies. These sounds, which are both deep and soothing, create an environment that is good for healing. When combined with the way crystals naturally vibrate, the effects are nothing short of life-changing.

Each crystal has a different lattice structure that makes it vibrate at a certain frequency. When these frequencies line up with the waves made by instruments used for sound healing, the healing benefits are amplified. Think of it as if two instruments were playing together in perfect balance, each adding to the melody of the other.

Think about the Rose Quartz, which is a stone of love. During a sound healing treatment, when it is placed close to the heart chakra, its gentle, loving energy gets turned on. Now, add the soothing sound of a sound bowl that has been tuned to match the frequency of the heart chakra. This combo makes for a very deep immersion. The vibrations of the sound bowl clean and activate the Rose Quartz, and the Rose Quartz, in turn, amplifies and directs the healing wishes of the sound waves right into the heart chakra. What happened? A deep feeling of inner freedom and heart-centered renewal.

The combination of sound therapy and crystal treatment can also be changed to fit different goals. There are crystals and sound frequencies that can help you think more clearly, feel more grounded, keep your emotions in check, or open your spiritual side. The key is to understand how each crystal is different and match it with the right waves of sound.

In the end, the union of sound healing and crystals is a dance of forces that works well together. Each mode is powerful on its own, but when they are used together, their power increases by a factor of ten. This combination is a holistic way to heal because it works on both the energetic and emotional levels. This makes sure that people leave the session feeling truly restored and in balance.

YOGA AND CRYSTALS

Yoga, which has been around for thousands of years, is a way to bring the mind, body, and spirit together. Through a series of postures, breathing exercises, and meditation techniques, it gives a journey of self-discovery and overall well-being. On the other hand, crystals, which are gifts from nature that come from deep within the Earth, have their own powers that can make different things better. When the ancient knowledge of yoga meets the resonating frequencies of crystals, the spiritual journey becomes much deeper and more meaningful.

Each asana or yoga pose is meant to free up energy, bring balance to the body and mind, and remove blocks. By adding crystals to this practice in a smart way, yoga practitioners can target certain chakras or energy centers, which makes the effects even stronger. For example, when doing grounding poses, which are meant to connect the yogi to the Earth and keep their energy stable, putting a Smoky Quartz near the mat can make these benefits stronger. This grounding stone, which is known for its ability to get rid of bad energy and make you feel more connected to the Earth, fits right in with the spirit of these poses.

On the other end of the spectrum, Lapis Lazuli can help with meditative asanas that aim for clarity, intuition, and a link to a higher consciousness. This deep blue stone is thought to help people reach enlightenment and make their dreams more vivid. If you hold it close during meditation, it can make it easier to connect with your inner knowledge.

Still, it's not just about sitting on a mat and meditating. Putting crystals all over the yoga space, from the sides of the room to the altar, can make it feel more energetic. This energy in the air can help you set intentions, relax more deeply, and make sure the yoga area stays clean and calm.

But even though yoga and crystals together have a lot of promise, it's important to approach this combination with knowledge and respect. Yoga and crystal treatment are both very big fields with long histories and lots of different parts. If you want to combine the two, it's important to spend time learning about the specific qualities of each crystal, the goals of each yoga pose, and how the two work together.

The way yoga and crystals are used together shows how beautiful holistic treatment can be. By using the best parts of both realms, practitioners can give and experience a deeper, richer path to balance, self-awareness, and spiritual growth. As always, what matters most is respect, understanding, and the never-ending search for ways to fit together well.

8

CRYSTAL HEALING FOR THE YOUNG SOULS:

Crystals for Children

8.1 INTRODUCING CRYSTALS TO CHILDREN

Children are naturally curious and open-minded, which makes them receptive to the forces in their environment. Their clear minds and pure souls make it easy for them to connect with the crystals' subtle vibrations. But to introduce these beautiful stones to young minds, you need to be gentle, patient, and a little creative.

When telling kids about crystal healing, it's important to look at things from their point of view. Children are naturally interested in the world and ask questions because they want to learn more about it. Start by telling them about crystals in a way that is simple and easy for them to understand. Talk to them about how these beautiful stones come from the heart of the Earth and how each one has its own energy to make people feel good and curious.

Children do best when they can use all of their abilities and learn by doing. Encourage them to touch, look at, and play with rocks to spark their curiosity and creativity. Set up a "crystal treasure hunt" or let them use different stones to make art. Children form a personal link with crystals through these hands-on activities, which helps them stay interested in the world's natural wonders for the rest of their lives.

UNDERSTANDING THEIR WORLD

Before diving into the world of crystal healing, it's essential to get into the child's shoes. Kids are curious by nature, and their questions stem from a genuine desire to understand. Begin by explaining crystals in simple terms that a child can grasp. Discuss how these beautiful stones come from deep within the Earth and carry special energies that can make us feel good.

MAKE IT INTERACTIVE

Children learn best when they can touch, feel, and play. Allow them to explore different crystals, noticing their textures, shapes, and colors. Maybe set up a "crystal treasure hunt" or let them create artwork with a selection of stones. Activities like these can foster a personal connection between the child and the crystals.

STORYTELLING

Young minds love stories. Weave tales about where each crystal comes from and what "powers" they hold. For instance, Rose Quartz could be a stone from a magical mountain that teaches people to love and care. Amethyst might be a piece of the night sky that fell to the Earth to help kids have sweet dreams. Through such narratives, children can form a deeper emotional bond with the crystals.

SAFETY FIRST

While children may be eager to explore, it's essential to ensure safety. Always supervise them around smaller crystals to avoid accidental ingestion. Additionally, educate them about the difference between "play" stones and "healing" stones, emphasizing that not all crystals should be placed in their mouths or carried in their pockets without supervision.

RESPECT THEIR INTUITION

Children have an uncanny ability to intuitively select crystals that resonate with their current needs. Observe and ask them about their choices. It's likely that they'll naturally gravitate towards a stone that aligns with their energetic needs.

Getting crystals for kids is a great way to encourage their natural sense of wonder and their natural interest in healing powers. By taking a hands-on, safe, and perfectly in tune with their world approach, you set the stage for a lifelong link to the beautiful and healing powers of nature's precious gems.

It's like giving a gift that keeps on giving to young people when you get them interested in crystals. You can teach children to appreciate the beauty and wonder of nature for the rest of their life by allowing them to explore, play with, and interact with these lovely stones. This introduction can play a vital role in their development by feeding their hearts and improving their understanding of the outside world.

8.2 BEST CRYSTALS FOR YOUNG ENERGY AND PROTECTION

When choosing crystals for young minds and hearts, the goal is frequently to nurture their energy and offer a safe haven in their developing environment. The following gems provide a sense of security while fostering their inner curiosity. They act as guardians of positivity and discovery.

AMETHYST

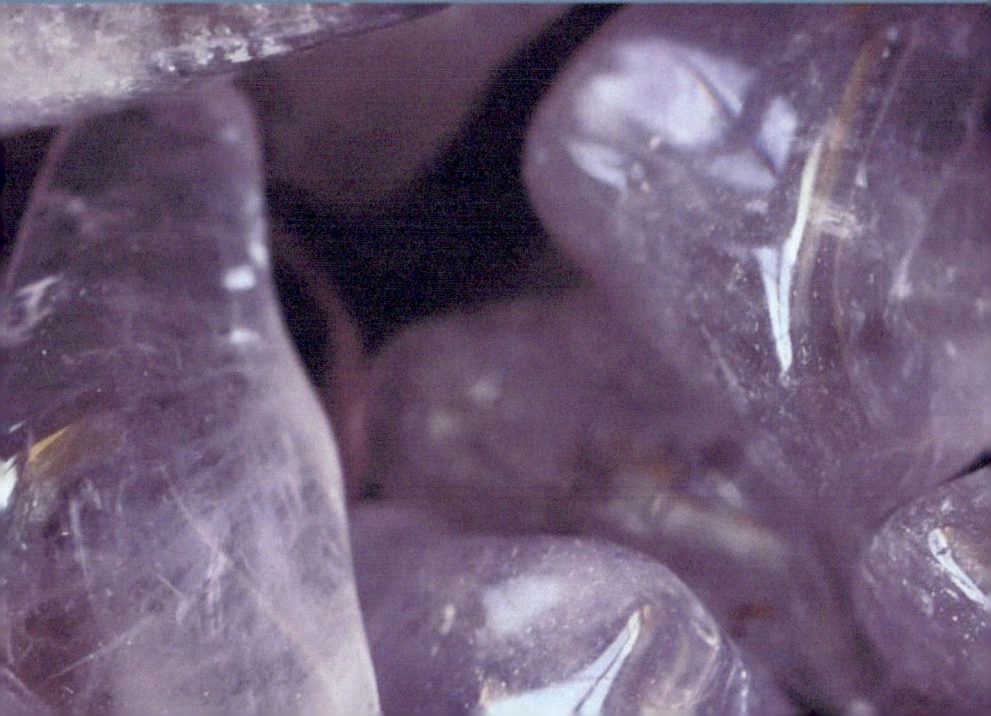

AMETHYST

Amethyst, with its deep purple and lilac colors that are mesmerizing, stands out as a source of peace and security for young souls just starting out on their journey of discovery. Deeply in tune with the soothing vibrations of the Earth, this crystal acts as a soft shield against the challenges of developing feelings, especially nightmares, anxiety, and the strange fears that can sometimes cloud a child's world.

Amethyst is very important as a sleep friend. People have said that this stone's gentle energies create an air of peace around the place where they rest, making it a peaceful haven. Putting an amethyst under their pillow or carefully placing it near their bed not only helps them get rid of worries at night, but it also makes it easier for them to get deep, restful sleep. As the child sleeps at night, the soothing vibrations of the crystal make sure he or she has nice dreams and wakes up with more energy in the morning.

By putting amethyst in a child's room, parents and other caretakers can give them more peace. In its quiet wisdom, this crystal wraps them in a gentle hug and promises them peaceful nights and a place where their innocent spirit can grow.

ROSE QUARTZ

ROSE QUARTZ

Rose quartz is often called the "Stone of Universal Love." It has a soft pink glow that represents the purest love and mental calm. This crystal is known for its ability to heal deep emotional wounds. It is a nurturing force that gently encourages the core values of kindness, self-love, and empathy in the person who holds it. Rose Quartz is a guiding light for young minds who are on the edge of life's vast emotional landscape. It helps them grow and understand their emotions in a real way.

When the Rose Quartz is put in a child's personal sanctuary, such as their room or favorite spot, it works hard to balance the energies around it and infuse them with feelings of warmth, acceptance, and tenderness. The aura it produces is like a cocoon, protecting the child from harm from the outside and letting them grow up in a loving environment. When worn as a pendant close to the heart, Rose Quartz also works as a lighthouse, reminding the wearer of the constant love that surrounds them. This helps them develop a strong heart that loves deeply and with empathy.

In the end, Rose Quartz is more than just a pretty stone; it's a friend who knows how complicated a young heart can be. By incorporating it into their lives, parents give their children an unspoken promise: that of endless love, understanding, and a gentle push toward becoming empathetic souls in this big world.

When the Rose Quartz is put in a child's personal sanctuary, such as their room or favorite spot, it works hard to balance the energies around it and infuse them with feelings of warmth, acceptance, and tenderness. The aura it produces is like a cocoon, protecting the child from harm from the outside and letting them grow up in a loving environment. When worn as a pendant close to the heart, Rose Quartz also works as a lighthouse, reminding the wearer of the constant love that surrounds them. This helps them develop a strong heart that loves deeply and with empathy.

In the end, Rose Quartz is more than just a pretty stone; it's a friend who knows how complicated a young heart can be. By incorporating it into their lives, parents give their children an unspoken promise: that of endless love, understanding, and a gentle push toward becoming empathetic souls in this big world.

CLEAR QUARTZ

CLEAR QUARTZ

Because of its many uses, clear quartz, also referred to as the "Master Healer," stands out among crystals. Its apparent elegance conceals a profound power that is capable of boosting vigor, enhancing focus, and dispelling the occasional mental fog that affects young people. Its resonance is thought to capture the very essence of clarity, acting as a mirror to reflect, amplify, and focus attention where it is most required.

Clear Quartz stands out as a useful tool in the context of a child's changing world, where they are continuously absorbing information and navigating new experiences. By placing a point of this crystal within their study area, it not only raises the space's vibrational frequency but also creates an environment that is conducive to concentration and learning. The young mind can fully immerse itself in the pleasures of learning because of the energy's ability to cut through distractions.

Furthermore, kids who have a piece of clear quartz in their pocket have a talisman at their disposal that constantly works to ward off negativity and improve their spirits. This crystal acts as a silent supporter, encouraging optimism and rational thought at every turn, whether they are tackling a difficult math issue or navigating playground politics. Children who have Clear Quartz at their side have a resource that helps them with their academic goals and promotes a constantly optimistic outlook on life.

BLACK TOURMALINE

BLACK TOURMALINE

Having a safety net becomes essential in the constantly changing world of childhood, when every turn offers new surprises and challenges. Here is where the dark earth tones of black tourmaline leave an enduring impression. This stone, which is well known for its grounding qualities, securely attaches youthful spirits to the Earth and makes sure they stay grounded even while they travel through uncharted territory, whether physically or emotionally.

Beyond its ability to ground, Black Tourmaline is renowned for being a strong defender. Its distinctive crystalline structure serves as an energy fortress, capable of fending off pressures that could try to stifle a child's inherent sense of adventure. The presence of this stone provides a reassuring comfort, whether it's protecting from the rare schoolyard fight or fending off excessive concerns.

We give children an ever-vigilant guardian by urging them to carry a piece of Black Tourmaline in their pocket or backpack. This small but potent talisman is prepared to ward off evil forces, giving our young explorers protection and confidence as they forge their individual course through the world. In addition to being protected, Black Tourmaline serves as a constant reminder of the perseverance and strength that are already a part of them.

CITRINE

CITRINE

Citrine, often likened to a sunlit drop of joy, is truly a beacon of hope and optimism in the world of gemstones. Its vibrant golden hues encapsulate the very essence of positivity, mirroring the brightness of a child's spirit. At the heart of this radiant stone lies the promise of abundance, not just in material wealth, but more importantly, in happiness, clarity, and the richness of experiences.

For young minds standing at the precipice of discovery and creativity, Citrine emerges as an invaluable ally. Its inherent properties bolster self-confidence, unlocking reservoirs of creativity often waiting to burst forth. Whether it's a daunting school project or the birth of a new hobby, the supportive energy of Citrine can pave the way for heightened motivation and unwavering dedication.

Strategically placing this crystal on a child's study desk or in their favorite workspace can have transformative effects. The surrounding environment becomes charged with Citrine's luminescent energy, turning routine tasks into invigorating endeavors. It serves as a gentle reminder that within each young soul lies boundless potential, waiting to be harnessed and celebrated. With Citrine's glowing embrace, every undertaking becomes an opportunity to shine brighter and bolder.

AMAZONITE

AMAZONITE

Communication and self-expression are like a complicated dance that kids and teens do as they grow up. As they find their voice in the noise of growing up, Amazonite stands as a steady guide, its soothing blue-green colors echoing the slow rise and fall of understanding. This gem, which is often compared to the calm waters of an unspoiled river, uses the power of both the throat chakra and the heart chakra to create a smooth connection between thought and words.

Amazonite is a peaceful stone that helps young people find their way in. It makes sure that when they say what they think, they say it with a mix of confidence and kindness, which makes their words both powerful and kind. The stone is a gentle reminder of how important it is to be true to yourself when you talk. It encourages them to speak their truths, even when peer pressure seems too strong.

By wearing an Amazonite bracelet or keeping a small piece in their pocket, kids and teens have a physical way to talk to each other in an honest way. This constant friend acts both as a shield against mistakes and a booster for clarity and kindness. With Amazonite by their side, young people are better able to navigate the complicated terrain of social interactions and build relationships based on confidence and real connection.

SELENITE

SELENITE

In a world full of energy and things to do, the ethereal white light of Selenite shines as a sign of purity and peace for children's impressionable minds. This crystal is known for its clean, almost otherworldly look. It protects young spirits by keeping away any negative forces that might try to upset their delicate balance. Every tiny line on its surface tells a story of protection and peace, making sure that the place it graces will never be disturbed from the outside.

When a Selenite wand is put in a child's room or a place they love to play, it does more than just make the room look nice. It gives off a gentle, safe vibe that makes it a safe place for young minds to explore, dream, and make things.

In this peaceful bubble, they are encouraged to let their creativity fly, and the energy of the crystal wraps them in a soothing hug. It's like having a quiet guardian who is always watching over them and making sure that the noise of the world doesn't change their innocence or happiness.

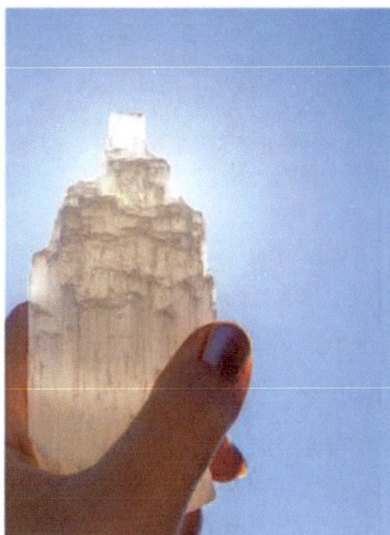

Introducing such powerful rocks to children is about more than just their physical health. It shows how much they want to give them tools that will help them grow and improve. As they hold or play with these gems, they are subtly led down a road of positivity, protection, and deep self-discovery. Each crystal's unique energy stays with them on their ever-changing trip, making sure they walk with confidence, grace, and a sense of wonder that never goes away.

CONCLUSION

Every moment, feeling, and thought we have sends out ripples of energy in our complex dance with the world. When we use the power of crystals, we're not just holding a beautiful piece of nature; we're also tapping into a force that has been building up for thousands of years. With its unique lattice and structure, each crystal sings a song of reverberation that touches us deeply.

Raising our vibrational frequency isn't just metaphysical jargon; it's a sign of how much we naturally want balance, health, and harmony. When we ask a crystal for help, we are basically admitting that we have a deep connection to nature and the world. We want crystals not just because they look nice, but also because we have a "vibrational match" with them. It's as if the world, in its infinite wisdom, has given us tools that sound like our own heartbeats and help us reach a place of peace and clarity.

As we come to the end of this book, I really hope that the pages you've read have shown you the mystery and beauty of crystals. This book is more than just a guide; it's an invitation to go on a trip that will change you, one that is filled with healing, empowerment, and deep self-discovery. As you learn more about crystal healing, you should always let your instincts be your guide. Keep your heart and mind open to the universe's many energies and lessons. Here is where the real magic of crystals lies, ready to be unlocked by souls looking for balance, healing, and a deeper connection with the universe.

BONUS

HOW TO CRAFT YOUR OWN CRYSTAL GRID

Crystal grids are powerful tools that amplify intentions by utilizing the combined energies of the crystals within them. For many, crafting a grid becomes an intuitive process where one is led by inner guidance. However, it's also helpful to have a clear guide, especially when starting out. In this bonus chapter, we'll dive deeper into the process of creating and using crystal grids for a variety of purposes.

1. THE BASICS OF A CRYSTAL GRID

A crystal grid is a complex arrangement of many crystals that have been precisely arranged in a predetermined geometric design. The grid's functionality depends heavily on its design, which serves more purposes than merely aesthetics. The layout's geometry acts as a conduit, allowing the natural energies of the crystals to flow through it and combine to form a stronger, more cohesive force.

These crystals' unique energies combine when they are arranged in this arrangement, creating a higher vibrational frequency that is strongly in tune with the cosmos. With the help of the user's intention and this increased energy, it is possible to manifest particular goals, heal, or even meditate. Your intentions are amplified by the grid, which then broadcasts them more strongly than they would otherwise.

MASTER STONE

The central stone, which acts as the main energy conduit. This stone is pivotal, setting the tone for the entire grid and channeling the primary energy source.

WAY STONES

These direct energy from the Master Stone outward. They serve as bridges, ensuring a smooth flow of energy from the central stone to the outermost parts of the grid.

DESIRE STONES

Situated on the outer grid, these help in manifesting your goals. They embody the specific outcomes or desires you hope to achieve, transforming the grid's energy into tangible results.

When setting up a crystal grid, it's important to remember that feeling is a big part of the process. Even though the above tips give you a framework, you should always go with your gut when picking and placing crystals. This personal touch not only makes the grid your own, but also makes the connection between you and the forces you're working with stronger.

2. CRAFTING A BASIC CRYSTAL GRID

STEP 1: CHOOSE A PURPOSE

Begin by determining the specific purpose of your grid. This could range from healing emotional wounds and guarding against negative energies, to attracting prosperity and abundance. Being clear on your intention will guide you in selecting the most appropriate crystals and help direct your energy during the activation process.

STEP 2: SELECTING CRYSTALS

After pinpointing your purpose, choose crystals that resonate with your specific intention. For instance, rose quartz is known for love and emotional healing, while citrine can be used for manifesting abundance. Do a bit of research or consult crystal reference guides to find the right ones for your needs.

STEP 3: CRYSTAL CLEANSE

Before placing them on the grid, cleanse each crystal. This ensures that any lingering energies from previous uses or handlers are cleared away. You can cleanse them using methods such as smudging with sage, moonlight bathing, or running them under natural water.

STEP 4: PICKING THE RIGHT SPOT

Find a quiet and calm space in your home or workspace to set up your grid. This space should be somewhere it won't be easily disturbed, allowing the grid to maintain its energy and focus. It's also beneficial if this is a place you frequent, so you're constantly reminded of your intentions.

STEP 5: SETTING THE MASTER STONE

Place your chosen Master Stone in the grid's center. This stone serves as your grid's energy focal point, directing and amplifying the energies of the surrounding crystals.

STEP 6: ARRANGING WAY STONES

Around the Master Stone, position your Way Stones in a geometric pattern or arrangement that feels right to you. These stones play a crucial role in directing energy outwards and bridging the energy between the Master Stone and the Desire Stones.

STEP 7: POSITIONING DESIRE STONES

On the outer edges of your grid, place the Desire Stones. These are representative of the specific outcomes or manifestations you hope to achieve with the grid. Their position ensures they are charged with the combined energies of all the other stones.

STEP 8: ACTIVATION

Finally, to activate your grid, take a clear quartz point and visualize your intention as you move it over the grid, often in a circular or connecting pattern. Imagine a flow of energy being channeled through the quartz, interlinking the crystals, and amplifying your grid's overall power.

3. TEMPLATES FOR CRYSTAL GRID CREATION

The arrangement of your crystals can be as important as the crystals themselves. Specific patterns or templates resonate with unique energies and can be tailored to align with your specific intention.

HERE ARE SOME DEEPER INSIGHTS INTO A FEW POPULAR CRYSTAL GRID TEMPLATES:

SPIRAL GRID

The spiral is a fundamental pattern found throughout nature and the universe, from galaxies to DNA helices. By emulating this pattern in a crystal grid, you tap into the primal energy of creation and evolution. A Spiral Grid is especially useful for those on a path of spiritual growth, personal transformation, or enlightenment. As you place each stone in the spiral formation, visualize your journey, starting from the center and expanding outwards, much like the journey of life and expansion of consciousness.

STAR GRID

Stars have long been symbols of hope, dreams, and aspirations. A Star Grid taps into this celestial energy, acting as a beacon for your desires. When creating a Star Grid, think of each point of the star as a beacon for your dreams. As you place each point, imbue it with a specific wish or aspiration. This grid is especially powerful for manifesting dreams, achieving goals, or illuminating your path forward.

CROSS GRID

The cross, a symbol rooted deep in history, represents the four cardinal directions and the four elements (earth, water, air, fire). This grid is about grounding and protection. When laying out a Cross Grid, see it as a compass, guiding and protecting you. Start with the central stone, representing the core of your being and your intention.

Then, as you lay each arm of the cross, align it with a specific direction, inviting protection, grounding, and balance from each corner of the universe.

This grid is particularly beneficial for those feeling scattered, seeking protection, or needing to anchor themselves in their current environment.

4. DIVERSE USES OF CRYSTAL GRIDS

SENDING HEALING

To transmit healing energy to a situation or person, visualize the recipient when activating the grid.

IN TREATMENT ROOMS

Place a grid in a therapy or treatment room to amplify the healing environment. A grid focusing on calm and balance, for instance, could use amethyst and selenite.

FOR CHILDREN'S BEDROOMS

Crafting a protective and calming grid using stones like rose quartz and black tourmaline can ensure peaceful sleep and positive dreams.

5. TIPS FOR EFFECTIVE GRIDS

CONSISTENCY IS KEY

Regularly reactivating your grid strengthens its power.

TRUST YOUR INTUITION

Allow your inner guidance to lead you in crystal placement.

CLEAR SPACE

Ensure the space around your grid is free of clutter, enhancing energy flow.

Keep in mind that the creation of a crystal grid is as unique as the individual who does it. The energies of the cosmos will align with your desires if you have faith in your intuition and the strength of your intentions. The combination of intention, energy, and geometric design makes a grid a powerful tool of manifestation and healing, whether you're making it for your own benefit or the benefit of others.

AUTHOR

Hi, I'm Kaya Slater and I am delighted you chose to read this book. I really do hope you enjoyed it as much as I enjoyed writing it!

If you found it helpful and supportive on your journey of health and wellness then please help me to reach others by sharing a review on Amazon, your review is invaluable in others receiving this wisdom and I am SO grateful to you for your support.

Please connect with me directly via my website anytime - **www.innerjourneywithkaya.com**

Made in United States
Troutdale, OR
03/06/2025

29557394R00102